retouching photos
in photoshop
elements 4

Visual QuickProject Guide

by Nolan Hester

Peachpit
Press

Visual QuickProject Guide
Retouching Photos in Photoshop Elements 4
Nolan Hester

Peachpit Press

1249 Eighth Street
Berkeley, CA 94710
510/524-2178
800/283-9444
510/524-2221 (fax)

Find us on the Web at: www.peachpit.com
To report errors, please send a note to errata@peachpit.com
Peachpit Press is a division of Pearson Education

Editor: Nancy Davis
Production Coordinator: David Van Ness
Compositor: David Van Ness
Proofreader: Tracy D. O'Connell
Indexer: Emily Glossbrenner
Cover design: Peachpit Press, Aren Howell
Interior design: Elizabeth Castro
Interior photos: Nolan Hester (except as noted in Special Thanks on page iv)
Cover photo credit: Photodisc

ISBN 0-321-41248-6

9 8 7 6 5 4 3 2 1

Printed and bound in the United States of America

This one's for Laika, a true-eyed soul.

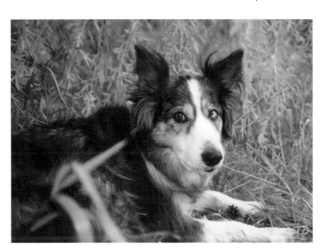

Special Thanks to...

Nancy Davis, my beyond-the-call editor, wise counsel, and friend.

David Van Ness for his deft layouts and calm amid my bookmaking storms.

Nancy Aldrich-Ruenzel, Peachpit's publisher, for making this work-from-home life possible.

And, as always, Mary.

Finally, my thanks to the friends who so kindly let me use their great photos: Ray Montoya (page 3), and Amy and Kelly Oliver (pages 65–66). My heart-felt appreciation also goes to everyone who appears in these photos: the entire Engel clan, Bruce Hammel, Nancy Harbert, Kerry Harder, plus Joshua, Jacob, and Soli. Thanks as well to the beauty of the Colorado Plateau, eastern France, New England, and to New Orleans— may she rise again.

contents

contents

introduction

The Visual QuickProject Guide that you hold in your hands offers a unique way to learn about new technologies. Instead of drowning you in theoretical possibilities and lengthy explanations, this Visual QuickProject Guide uses big, color illustrations coupled with clear, concise step-by-step instructions to show you how to complete each photo retouching project in less than an hour.

In this book you'll be retouching your photos using Adobe Photoshop Elements 4, one of the most powerful, yet easy to use image editing programs available. Each chapter walks you through fixing some of the most common—and often bedeviling—problems you'll encounter when working on your photos. By the end of the book, you'll not only know how to deal with these problems, you'll also understand which tools work best in each situation and how to work quickly and efficiently.

Aside from Adobe Photoshop Elements 4, your Windows computer must be running Microsoft Windows XP Professional or Home Edition with Service Pack 2.

Adobe has improved Photoshop Elements 4 with lots of little tweaks. Major new features are highlighted with **NEW**. Examples include the Magic Selection Brush (page 54) and the Magic Extractor Tool (page 101).

You'll find all the example files used in the book—including before and after versions of the photos—at this book's companion site http://www.waywest. net/psevqj/. The site also includes corrections for any mistakes that might be found after the book was printed.

you'll create

These two pages represent just some of the photo problems you'll learn how to solve.

Use Elements to quickly fix red eye, a common problem when photographing people with a flash at night or in a darkened room. (See page 19.)

The Auto button, found in the Quick Fix mode, lets you quickly rebalance an over- or under exposed photo. (See page 28.)

The Standard Edit mode's various tools gives you far more precise control over a photo's shadows and high-lights. (See page 54.)

Easily restore distorted skin tones by adjusting Saturation, Hue, Temperature, and Lightness. (See page 69.)

Rescue torn or faded heirloom photos with some of the advanced tools in Elements. (See page 85.)

Stitch together a series of side-by-side photos to create wonderfully detailed panoramas that look great as large prints. (See page 111.)

introduction

how this book works

The title explains what is covered in that section.

Significant new features in Photoshop Elements 4 are highlighted with **NEW** to alert users of earlier versions of Photoshop Elements.

extract & defringe objects

NEW In the previous section, we carefully removed just the wires while preserving the blue sky. But suppose, we wanted to remove all the sky and work only with the remaining sign and building? The new Magic Extractor is perfect for that sort of task, especially since it includes a Defringe option to automatically remove the boundary fringe of pixels often mistakenly selected with an object. (See extra bits on page 115.)

Numbered steps lead you through the sequence of actions, showing only the details you really need.

1 Open a photo from which you want to extract a particular area. In our example, we'll start by opening the same wire-free photo we created on pages 98–100. Choose Image > Magic Extractor and the image appears within the Magic Extractor dialog box.

2 The Foreground Brush Tool will be selected by default with a Brush Size of 20 pixels.

Screenshots focus on what part of Elements you'll be using for the particular project step.

3 Click within the photo on all the areas you want to add to your selection. Each of the areas will be marked by a red dot.

Names of Elements tools, palettes, and any crucial concepts are shown in orange.

repair & transform photos

101

The extra bits section at the end of each chapter contains additional tips and tricks that you might need to know. Read them in tandem with the particular page you're working on.

fix skin tone with mask

extra bits

The heading for each group of tips matches the section title. (The colors are just for decoration and have no hidden meaning.)

set color management p. 62
- The Always Optimize Colors for Computer Screens choice makes the most sense when you're creating onscreen slide shows, photos for emailing, posting on the Web, and even ordering prints online. If, however, you always create photos for your own local (desktop) printer then choose Always Optimize for Printing.

adjust with variations p. 65
- It's common to bounce between the Midtones and Saturation choices in the Color Variations dialog box.
- If you have a faded print or slide try boosting the saturation in the Variations dialog box.

fix hue with layer p. 67
- You can readjust the hue/saturation any time by double-clicking the adjustment layer.
- If you want more control, click in the number text window and use the ↑ or ↓ keys to change the number one digit at a time. Use Shift↑ or Shift↓ to move in 10-digit steps.

fix skin tone p. 69
- Feel free to try the new Enhance > Adjust Color > Adjust Color for Skin Tone feature on page 32. In this example, that feature fixed the skin tones—but skewed the color of the flowers.
- With a mask, you can adjust the color and exposure. Depending on which layer you select, you can apply color/lighting changes to the Background or Background copy.
- Depending on the photo, it may be quicker to create the layer mask using the Magic Selection Brush Tool (see page 54–55).

remove color noise p. 74
- The remove color noise feature also can be a lifesaver if you're using a low-resolution camera phone. Faces in particular can wind up looking splotchy.

warm or cool colors p. 76
- While you could apply a warming or cooling filter to the photo's Background layer, the adjustment layer preserves your original pixels.
- Whether you're warming or cooling a photo, feel free to readjust the Density slider from the standard 25 percent. For a realistic effect, keep it below 40 percent.

Next to the heading there's a page number that also shows which section the tips belong to.

80
adjust colors

the next step

This Visual QuickProject Guide focuses on fixing common exposure problems, repairing damaged photos, a few cool transformation tricks, and then sharing the results with friends and family. It does not dive deep into all the amazing tools and filters packed into Elements. If you want to learn more about them, try Photoshop Elements 4 for Windows: Visual QuickStart Guide, by Craig Hoeschen.

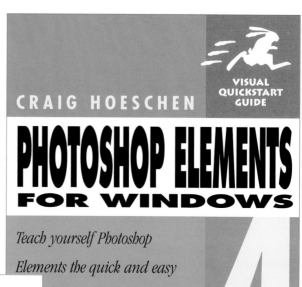

CRAIG HOESCHEN

VISUAL QUICKSTART GUIDE

PHOTOSHOP ELEMENTS
FOR WINDOWS

Teach yourself Photoshop

Elements the quick and easy

́ This Visual QuickStart

e uses pictures rather than

hy explanations. You'll be

nd running in no time!

4

Creative Techniques

Figure 12.77 This final composite image was created from two separate images.

Figure 12.78 Here, I used a picture of a boy and a photograph of space to create an otherworldly image.

Figure 12.79 Use the Background Eraser tool (or any other selection tool) to isolate your source image.

Creating whimsical composite images

In many cases, as in the previous example, you composite images to improve them in a way that isn't obvious to the viewer. You don't want to draw attention to your work; you just want to improve the image (as in the ship and sky example). But sometimes you want your audience to wonder how you created that cool special effect. This composite for an elementary school astronomy fair poster is an image that looks pretty realistic, if a little fantastical (**Figure 12.77**). (See the color plate section of this book for a full-color view of this task.)

To combine images:

1. Open two images that you want to composite (**Figure 12.78**).

2. Use the selection tools and/or eraser tools to isolate part of the source image. In this case, we'll use the Background Eraser tool to erase the background from the boy, leaving the area around him transparent (**Figure 12.79**). This way, he'll insert nicely into the target image, with no messy halos or edges around his body.

3. Copy the area of the source image that you want to composite.

continues on next page

COMPOSITING IMAGES

391

The Visual QuickStart Guide teaches you step-by-step how to use every aspect of Elements. Its 400-plus pages are packed with clear examples and helpful tips. Like all the books in Peachpit's Visual QuickStart Guide series, it also works as a reference guide when you just need to learn (or remember) the steps for completing a task.

1. getting ready

Part of what makes taking digital photos so much fun is that you can immediately see if you got the shot. Using Adobe Photoshop Elements, you're about to discover the other part of the digital fun: It's easy to make good shots great. You'll learn how to tweak your photos so that they pop off the screen and page. You'll fix not-quite-perfect shots faster than any darkroom technician. And you'll double your skills to create eye-catching photos to share with your family and friends This chapter's quick overview will get you going. Later chapters will cover all the details you'll need to know.

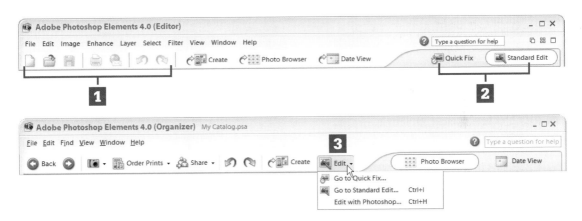

Here are, for example, the shortcuts bars for the Elements Editor (top) and Organizer (bottom). Beyond icons for such basic functions as opening, saving, printing, and undoing mistakes **1**, the Editor's shortcuts bar gives you a quick way to switch between Elements' Quick Fix and Standard Edit modes **2**. The Organizer's shortcuts bar includes buttons for navigating through your photos, ordering prints, sharing them, adding and removing organizing tags, creating multimedia items, and most importantly, switching back to the Editor's Quick Fix and Standard Edit modes **3**.

Welcome screen

When you first launch Elements from your desktop, the Welcome screen appears by default. (See extra bits on page 15.)

You can choose whether to work in the Quick Fix or Standard Edit mode of the Elements Editor. If you prefer, you can launch the Organizer, which offers an easy way to view all your photos and decide which ones need editing. (For more information on the Elements Editor, see the next page; for the Organizer, see page 4.)

If you are upgrading to Photoshop Elements 4 from version 3, you'll be asked if you want to convert your existing catalog of images. Click OK to begin the conversion, which can take several minutes depending on how many images you've previously catalogued using Elements.

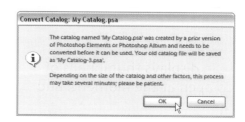

Elements Editor

The Elements Editor offers two modes: Quick Fix and Standard Edit. Quick Fix lets you make simple corrections for the most common photo problems. When you need more control—fine-tuning a particular aspect or changing a selected part of the photo—use Standard Edit.

In both edit modes, the Toolbox runs down the left side of the main window with the related Options Bar across the top of the window. Your choices in the Options Bar change depending on which tool you select.

By clicking either tab, you can jump between Quick Fix and Standard Edit.

In Quick Fix, the Palette Bin offers a few simple sliders to fix photos; the Standard Edit palette is packed with controls for more complex fixes. The Quick Fix palette is locked in place, but you can reposition every pane in the Standard Edit palette. (See arrange work space on page 6.)

The Photo Bin displays thumbnails of every photo open at the moment, and puts a blue border around the photo being displayed in the main window. Click another thumbnail to see that photo in the main window.

Elements Organizer

The Organizer gives you a way to quickly find, sort, and label all your photos. Its Photo Browser tab includes the Organizer Bin, which you can use to apply category/subject Tags to individual photos.

Click the drop-down menu to edit a selected photo in the Editor's Quick Fix or Standard Edit mode.

Click the Date View tab to find photos by when they were shot. (See next page.)

The main window displays all your photos or just those matching your search criteria (in this example, the New Orleans tag).

Click the drop-down menu to sort photos with newest first, oldest first, or group by import batch.

Move the slider to change the size of photos in the main window. Click the left button to shrink them as much as possible, the right button to zoom in on just one photo, or the far-right button to trigger a full-screen slide show of all photos in the main window.

Use the Tags tab and its tools to create and apply category/subject labels to photos.

Check boxes to find photos marked with that tag. Check multiple boxes to find photos marked with all those tags.

getting ready

The main Date View window uses thumbnail images to mark days when photos were shot. Use the buttons to move forward or back.

Click to select any day in the main window, or use the forward and back buttons to select another day.

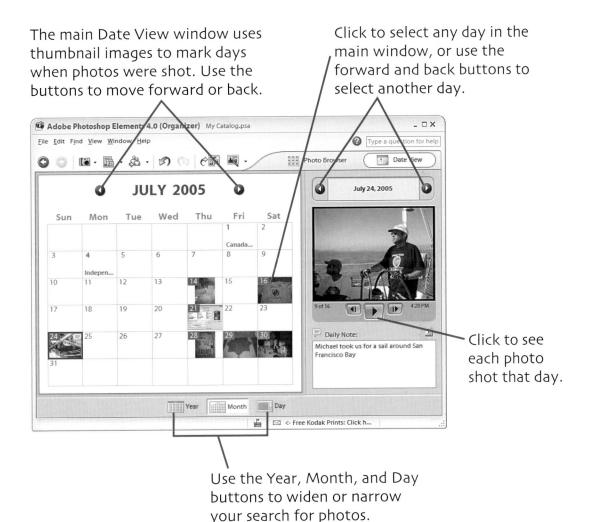

Click to see each photo shot that day.

Use the Year, Month, and Day buttons to widen or narrow your search for photos.

arrange work space

Digital cameras make it so easy to take lots of photos, you'll find yourself using Elements a lot. Make yourself at home—and work more efficiently—by arranging the Editor and Organizer work spaces just as you like. If you're using a laptop with a small screen, you'll find it helpful to collapse the Palette, Photo, and Organizer bins.

In either Quick Fix or Standard Edit mode, you can gain some screen real estate by collapsing the Photo Bin. Click the thin arrow-bar separating the main window from the Photo Bin below. Then, expand your photo to fill the larger main window by choosing [Ctrl][O]. To expand the Palette Bin back to its full size, click the bar again.

Here's another way to collapse or expand any of the bins: click the green arrow at the bottom of the bin. To restore the bin to its full size, just click the arrow again.

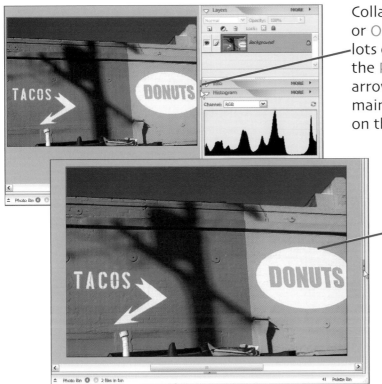

Collapsing the Palette Bin or Organizer Bin creates lots of elbow room. As with the Photo Bin, click the thin arrow-bar separating the main window from the bin on the right.

You can then use Ctrl O to expand your photo to fill the expanded main window.

Click the thin arrow-bar again to restore any bin.

arrange work space (cont.)

If you only need one or two palettes for the moment, why let the Palette Bin hog your screen? Instead, click the needed palette's top tab, and drag it to a new spot on top of the photo.

Now, collapse the Palette Bin as explained on page 7, and drag it to a new spot.

Then, expand your photo to take advantage of the extra space, using Ctrl O.

Finally, you can hide or reveal the details of any pane in the Editor, or tag in the Organizer, by clicking its triangular arrow.

getting ready

set & calibrate monitor

Most likely your monitor is already set to display colors at its highest quality, but it's best to make sure. Calibration is only possible if you're using a traditional monitor with a cathode ray tube (CRT). It's not practical for an LCD monitor (all laptops or any thin-flat external monitor) because the LCD's apparent brightness changes with your angle of view. (See extra bits on page 15 for a workaround.)

Choose Start > Control Panel > Display, and then click the Settings tab.

Make sure the Color quality panel is set to Highest (32 bit) or True Color (24 bit) and click OK to close.

To calibrate the monitor, choose Start > Control Panel > Adobe Gamma.

If Adobe Gamma is not a choice, do this instead: navigate here on your C hard drive (that's your main drive): ~\C:\Program Files\Common Files\Adobe\Calibration\ and double-click Adobe Gamma.

When the Adobe Gamma dialog box appears, choose Step By Step (Wizard), click Next, and follow the instructions.

get from Organizer

Thanks to its thumbnail images, the Organizer is often the easiest place to find a photo. So it's not surprising that you'll often find yourself wanting to open photos within the Organizer and then switch to the Editor to work on them. (see extra bits on page 16.)

1 If you're in the Editor, click Photo Browser in the Shortcuts bar.

2 If the Organizer is already running, it will appear immediately, otherwise a progress bar will appear while it launches.

3 You can then use your Tags, or any of the Organizer's many sort tools, to find the photo you want to fix.

4 Once you find the photo, right-click it and choose either Go to Quick Fix or Go to Standard Edit from the drop-down menu. The photo will then appear in the Elements Editor for retouching.

get from camera

Make sure your camera or loaded card-reader is connected. (If the Adobe Photo Downloader tries to take over the process, see extra bits on page 16.)

1 Switch from the Elements Editor to its Organizer by clicking the Photo Browser button in the shortcuts bar. When the Organizer appears, click the camera button in the shortcuts bar and choose From Camera or Card Reader in the drop-down menu.

2 Select your camera or card in the Get Photos from drop-down menu and click Get Photos.

get from camera (cont.)

3 The photos will be copied to your computer and a task bar will track their progress.

4 Elements will then automatically scan the photos you're importing for instances of red-eye. Just be aware that the dialog box will say it's fixing cases of red-eye even when, as with this landscape photo, there aren't any people.

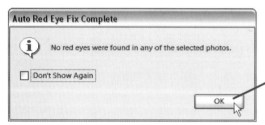

If you want to know if any eyes were fixed, look at this dialog box, which appears after all the photos are imported. Click OK and the photos will appear in the Organizer, where you can open them for retouching in the Editor. (See the third step in get from Organizer on page 10.) (See extra bits on page 16.)

getting ready

get from scanner

No doubt you have photos not shot with a digital camera that you'd like to fix. A scanner makes it simple to move prints onto your computer. If you've already used a program included with the scanner to import photos, then just follow the steps in get from Organizer on page 10.

1 To import scanner images directly into Elements, switch from the Editor to the Organizer by clicking the Photo Browser button in the shortcuts bar.

2 When the Organizer appears, click the camera button in the shortcuts bar and choose From Scanner in the drop-down menu. A progress bar will track the scanning. When the import is completed done, the photos will appear in the Organizer, where you can open them for retouching in the Editor. (See the third step in get from Organizer on page 10.)

reformat photos

Most digital cameras save photos as JPEG (or JPG) files because they're compact yet they capture lots of detail. Unfortunately, every time you resave a JPG file, which you'll do as you edit and re-edit, it throws away data. By saving your newly imported photos as TIFF files, you can retouch without losing crucial detail. Later, if you want to send out an email or Web version, Elements can automatically convert the TIFF. (See extra bits on page 16; share photos on page 117.)

1 Open the photo you want to reformat in the Editor and choose File > Save As. Click the Format drop-down menu to select TIFF, and then click Save.

2 In the TIFF Options dialog box, leave the compression set to NONE. Most recent image applications will be able to open the file whether the Byte Order is set to IBM PC or Macintosh, so the choice is yours. Leave everything else as it is and click OK. Now we're ready to start editing in the next chapter!

extra bits

Welcome screen p. 2

- If you want to bypass the Welcome screen and start up directly in the Editor view, click the drop-down menu in the bottom-left and select Editor. Uncheck the Show at Startup box, also at the bottom-left of the Welcome screen.

Elements Editor p. 3

- Clicking the Photo Browser button in the shortcuts bar lets you jump to the Elements Organizer. The Photo Browser, by the way, is not the same thing as the now-retired File Browser found in Elements 3.

set & calibrate monitor p. 9

- Many monitors now are self-calibrating, which makes this step unnecessary. Check your display's manual to make sure.

- If you're using an LCD monitor, open a photo file that has an even range of colors and tones, from bright to dark. Adjust the LCD's angle to minimize any glare or distortion in the image. (In contrast, if you crank the LCD nearly flat you'll see how it distorts the color of the image.) Similarly, work away from bright sun or windows when you're retouching your photos, since that will skew your perception of the image.

- If you're lucky enough to have a CRT and an LCD monitor, run the Elements Editor on the CRT screen for the best results.

extra bits

get from Organizer p. 10

- If you make a point of opening all your photos from within the Organizer, it will automatically keep track of your photos—no matter where they reside on your hard drive.

get from camera p. 11

- When you're getting photos, you may have to battle the Adobe Photo Downloader, which auto-launches whenever you connect a camera or load a flash card. For me, it adds an unwanted step. To disable it, open the Organizer preferences (Edit > Preferences > Camera or Card Reader) and uncheck Use Adobe Photo Down-loader.

- When Elements offers to erase your card after importing photos, click No to avoid accidentally erasing any photos. Reformat the card with your camera, not the computer.

- If you find the new auto red-eye fix feature a bother, you can turn it off by unchecking the box in the Options pane of the Get Photos dialog box.

reformat photos p. 14

- If you're lucky enough to have a newer, high-end digital camera that saves photos in the RAW format, use RAW since it's even better than using TIFF files.

- Be sure to check Include in the Organizer. The photo will be stored with all the other versions of the photo, no matter what their formats.

- Yes, it's tempting, but resist renaming all your images from their arbitrary numbers to some-thing you'll recognize. The whole point of date-and-keyword programs like the Organizer is to make it easy to find your photos, no matter what they're named.

2. make quick fixes

The Quick Fix mode helps you correct the most common—and easiest to solve—problems found in photos. Like the Quick Fix pane itself, this chapter starts with general items like rotating and red-eye, then makes lighting and color adjustments, and ends with sharpening. Always work in that order. If you apply sharpening first, for example, your results will not look as good.

Before any fixes, the top-left photo suffers from the usual problems: red-eye, too-dark shadows, overly bright highlights, and a slight color cast.

The lower-right version shows the fixes explained in this chapter. And the fixes really are quick: it only took two minutes to apply them all.

rotate photo

Digital cameras have become so good at sensing when you're shooting a vertical image that you rarely need to manually rotate photos. Still, there's always the exception. Photos can be rotated in Quick Fix mode or Standard Edit mode, though the buttons are available only in Quick Fix. (See extra bits on page 35.)

1 In the Organizer, select the photo you want to rotate, then open it with the Editor by right-clicking the photo and choosing Go to Quick Fix or Go to Standard Edit in the drop-down menu. (Ctrl I takes you directly to the Standard Edit mode.)

2 Click the rotate left or right button just below the main photo window.

3 A progress bar will appear briefly before the photo rotates 90 degrees. Repeat if necessary to properly orient the image.

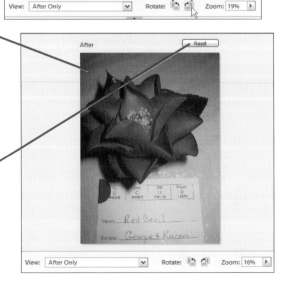

4 If you change your mind, click Reset and the image will return to its original orientation. Be sure to save your changes (Ctrl S).

make quick fixes

fix flash red eye

Take a flash shot of people in a darkened room and almost inevitably the centers of their eyes will appear blood red. Fortunately, this is easy to fix, especially with the new Auto Red Eye Fix. The red eye tool and technique work the same whether you're in Quick Fix mode or Standard Edit mode. (See extra bits on page 35.)

1 Open the photo you want to fix and set the drop-down menu in the main window to Before and After (Portrait).

2 Select the Zoom tool in the Toolbox.

4 If you need to recenter the eyes, use the Hand Tool.

3 Click in the After frame on the eyes that need to be fixed. Repeat until you can clearly see the red areas.

fix flash red eye (cont.)

5 Click the Toolbox's Red Eye Removal tool.

6 NEW Start by clicking Auto, which works amazingly well and just may save you from doing the rest of these steps. Two progress bars will appear briefly as the photo is scanned. If you're not happy with the results of the auto fix, click Reset and see the next step.

7 In the After frame, click and drag to select just one of the red eyes.

8 Release your cursor and the red will be removed. Repeat the same steps to remove red from the other eye.

9 If you're still not happy with the results, click Reset and see the next step.

10 The red eye tool sometimes needs a little help finding and removing all the red. By default, the red eye tool is set at 50-50 in the Options Bar, so it darkens exactly half of the pupil's size by half its original darkness (the photo equivalent of an F-stop).

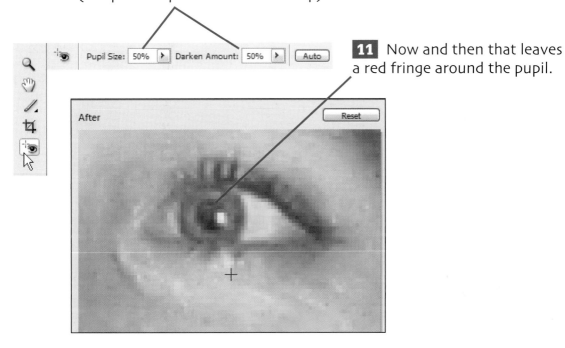

11 Now and then that leaves a red fringe around the pupil.

12 To fix it, click the Pupil Size drop-down menu in the tool's Options Bar and move the slider a little to the right.

13 If you find the tool is turning red eyes pinkish-gray instead of black, drag the Darken Amount slider to the right.

14 When you have finished reapplying the red eye fix, reset the tool, and it will return to the 50-50 default.

crop photo

Make a rough crop of your photos before you dive into fixing any exposure or color problems. After you've fixed everything else, you can then come back and make a second, final crop to put the borders exactly where you want them. (See extra bits on page 35.)

Open the photo you want to crop in either Quick Fix mode or Standard Edit mode.

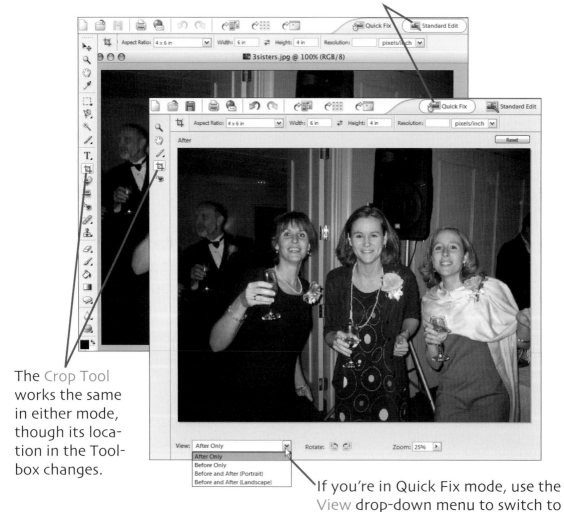

The Crop Tool works the same in either mode, though its location in the Toolbox changes.

If you're in Quick Fix mode, use the View drop-down menu to switch to any view other than Before Only, which won't let you crop.

If you'll eventually want prints of the photo, choose a crop ratio from the Aspect Ratio drop-down menu. In the example, we've chosen 4 x 6 in since that's the most popular print size. (For more on print sizes, see page 118.)

1 Click and drag in the main window, where your aspect ratio will be used as you position the crop box.

2 Release the cursor and, if necessary, click the Hand Tool if you need to reposition the overall position of the crop. (To switch back, click the Crop Tool again.)

3 To resize a particular side, click and drag any corner of the crop box.

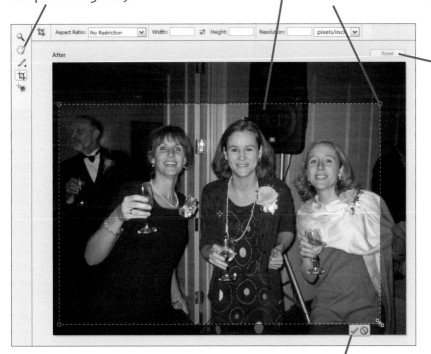

5 If you don't like the results, click Reset.

4 To apply the crop, double-click the photo or click the check mark.

make quick fixes

use Smart Fix

Smart Fix essentially lets you retouch a photo with a single click. If you don't like the effect, which applies a combination of lighting and color fixes, you can adjust the amount with the slider. If you need more control, see the fix lighting and fix colors sections on pages 28 and 31. (See extra bits on page 35.)

1 Open the photo you want to fix in Quick Fix mode and set the main window's drop-down menu to Before and After (and choose between Portrait or Landscape). Choose the one that best shows the main part of your photo, repositioning if necessary with the Hand and Zoom tools.

2 If the General Fixes pane isn't already show-ing in the Palette Bin, click its triangle.

3 Click Auto to apply the Smart Fix.

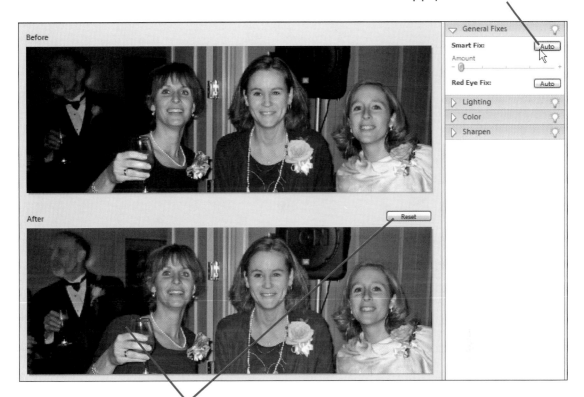

4 In the example, Smart Fix lightened the black dress a tad too much, making it look gray. We'll click Reset to cancel the effect.

make quick fixes

use Smart Fix (cont.)

5 Drag the Amount slider to find the best balance between lightening the dark areas without washing out the light areas.

6 Once you find the right spot for the slider, click the ✔ to apply the effect or press ⏎Enter.

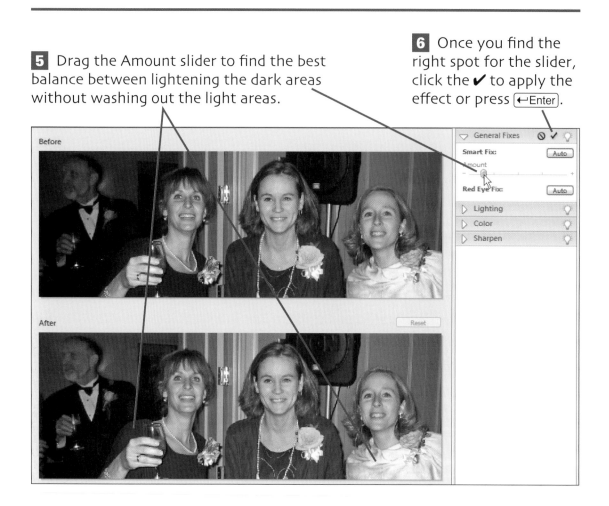

make quick fixes

match the light

Here's a quick bit of background before using the Quick Fix Lighting pane, which controls levels and contrast, two key aspects of your photo's exposure. Levels refer to a photo's overall mix of tones, from light (highlights) to midtones to dark (shadows). Contrast refers to the amount of difference between a photo's lightest and darkest tones.

In the stork photo on the left, there's so little contrast that it's all gray midtones with virtually no highlights or shadows.

The street-scene photo on the right has great contrast, but a skewed mix of lighting levels. Its shadows are too dark to show any detail, while the sun reflecting off the windows is so bright that the highlights are completely washed out.

In general, you want the mix of levels to match the light you saw when you took the shot. That mix, of course, varies from scene to scene. Night scenes naturally have more shadows, mid-day desert scenes more highlights. The Lighting pane cannot work miracles by resurrecting badly exposed photos like these two. But if you start with a halfway decent exposure, the Lighting pane can take your photo the rest of the way.

fix lighting

When using the Quick Fix Lighting pane, the Levels Auto button will adjust a photo's levels and color. The Contrast Auto button affects only the contrast and leaves the colors unchanged. Feel free to experiment: The difference can be subtle or dramatic, depending on your photo. But if you're happy with the colors, use Contrast Auto, as in the example below.

1 Open the photo you want to fix in Quick Fix mode and set the main window's drop-down menu to Before and After (and choose between Portrait or Landscape). Choose the one that best shows the main part of your photo, repositioning if necessary with the Hand and Zoom tools.

2 If the Lighting pane isn't already showing in the Palette Bin, click its triangle.

3 Click Auto to fix the contrast.

4 In the example, the Quick Fix does a pretty good job reducing the glare off Disney Hall's stainless steel while preserving shadow details. But we can do better.

make quick fixes

fix lighting (cont.)

5 By first dragging the Darken Highlights slider a tiny bit to the right, we take out the last bit of glare.

6 Now Lighten Shadows a bit by dragging that slider to the right. (In both cases, dragging to the right increases the effect; to the left reduces it.)

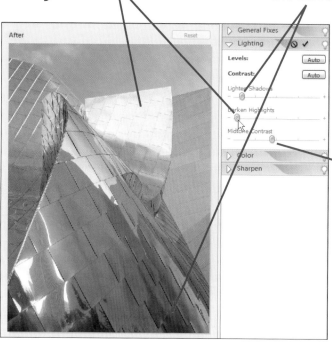

7 By moving the Midtone Contrast slider ever so slightly to the left, the steel's midtones lose any harshness. (This slider normally sits at the middle tick mark.)

8 That's much better than the original image, so apply the change by clicking the ✔ or pressing ↵Enter.

make quick fixes

fix colors

You'll find that Quick Fix does a fairly good job of adjusting colors. It does this by applying a neutral color cast to the photo's midtones, which is especially helpful if your photo looks too cool (blueish) or too warm (reddish). (See extra bits on page 36.)

1 Open the photo you want to fix in Quick Fix mode and set the main window's drop-down menu to Before and After (and choose between Portrait or Landscape). Choose the one that best shows the main part of your photo, repositioning if necessary with the Hand and Zoom tools.

2 If the Color pane isn't already showing in the Palette Bin, click its triangle.

3 Click Auto to fix the color.

4 If you're not happy with the results, click Reset to cancel the effect and see adjust colors on page 61 for a method that offers finer control over colors.

fix skin tones

NEW In Photoshop Elements 4 Adobe has greatly improved how well it adjusts skin tones to make them appear more natural by removing any blue or red tinge from the photo's overall color cast. Amazingly accurate, it takes the guess work out of what had been a frustratingly subtle adjustment.

1 Open the photo you want to fix in Standard Edit mode (Ctrl I) and set the main window's drop-down menu to Before and After (and choose between Portrait or Landscape). Position the photo so that you have a close view of a facial area.

2 From the Enhance menu, choose Adjust Color > Adjust Color for Skin Tone.

3 When the Adjust Color for Skin Tone dialog box appears, use the eye-dropper-shaped cursor to click a representative area of skin (neither flashed nor shadowed).

6 If you're happy with the results, click OK and save your changes (Ctrl S). If you want to start fresh with a different skin sample, click Reset.

4 Compare the photo's sometimes-subtle overall color shift in the After window to the Before window.

5 If necessary, use the Skin and Ambient Light sliders to further adjust the color.

make quick fixes

sharpen automatically

It's common for digital photos to lose a bit of sharpness as you work on them. The Sharpen pane helps fix that by increasing the contrast along the edges of objects. But be careful. Too much sharpening will make the photo look fake, as if the foreground objects are pasted onto the background.

1 Open the photo you want to sharpen in Quick Fix mode and set the main window's drop-down menu to Before and After (and choose between Portrait or Landscape). Avoid zooming in very much because you won't be able to accurately judge the effect of the sharpening.

2 If the Sharpen Pane isn't already showing in the Palette Bin, click its triangle. Click Auto to apply the sharpening. The effect should be subtle, adding just a bit of crispness.

sharpen automatically (cont.)

3 You can zoom in to see the effect at the pixel-by-pixel level.

4 By dragging the slider all the way to the right, you can clearly see the speckly distortion created by over sharpening.

5 To cancel, click Reset or the ⊘.

make quick fixes

extra bits

rotate photo p. 18

- To rotate images within Standard Edit mode, choose Image > Rotate and make a choice from the drop-down menu.

- Beyond the standard 90° and 180° button choices, you also can rotate a photo by just a few degrees—extremely handy if the horizon in your landscape shot is a bit crooked. From Quick Fix or Standard Edit modes, choose Image > Rotate > Custom and when the Rotate Canvas dialog box appears, enter a number in the Angle window and click OK.

fix flash red eye p. 19

- More and more digital cameras now have a red-eye reduction flash, which uses a blinking light to shrink the subject's pupil before firing the main flash. You also can reduce red eye by taking pictures at a slight angle to your subject's eyes.

- If you have Elements set to automatically fix red-eye as you import photos (see pages 11–12), then you generally won't need to manually fix red-eye in new photos. But you may still need the feature for any pre-version 4 flash photos in your Elements catalog.

- The red eye tool does not work as consistently if you select both eyes together.

crop photo p. 22

- If possible, it's best to crop your image before shooting by moving closer to your subject. The more you crop after you take the picture, the harder it becomes to produce a big print that's still sharp because, in effect, you're throwing away pixels.

- To cancel the crop before you apply it, click the Options Bar's ⊘ or press Esc.

use Smart Fix p. 24

- While you could use Smart Fix in Standard Edit mode by choosing Enhance from the menu bar, in this case using Quick Fix mode is better since you can compare Before and After views, as well as use the slider adjustment.

- Don't zoom in so close on your Before and After views that you can't see the overall effect of the Smart Fix.

- Clicking Auto repeatedly will only muddy the photo; hit Reset and start fresh.

extra bits

fix colors p. 31

- While the Color pane includes four sliders, they are too sensitive for subtle adjustments, such as skin tones. (For that, use the new fix skin tones feature on page 32.). But the color sliders can be fun for creating surreal colors in non-people photos. For finer control over colors other than skin tones, see adjust colors on page 61.

make quick fixes

3. correct exposures

Standard Edit mode offers far more control than Quick Fix mode for correcting a photo's exposure problems. By combining the Levels dialog box, adjustment layers, and a few items from the Toolbox, you can fix even the most challenging exposures.

undo multiple changes

When working in Quick Fix mode, the standard undo command ($\boxed{\text{Ctrl}}\boxed{\text{Z}}$) is all you need. But as you edit your photos in Standard Edit mode you'll quickly learn to appreciate the Undo History palette. As long as you haven't yet saved your edits, the palette lets you step back through all your changes. That frees you to plunge into photo editing's necessary trial-and-error process without fear.

1 In the menu bar, choose Window > Undo History and the Undo History palette will appear in the Palette Bin. If it appears instead as a free-floating palette, click the red button (in the upper right) and it will close and reappear within the Palette Bin.

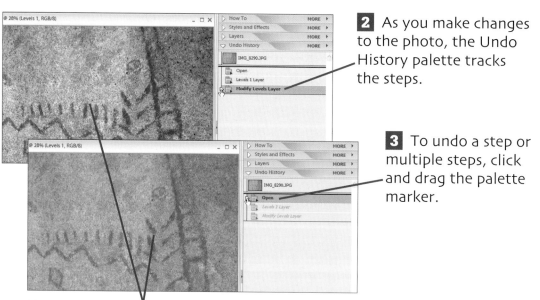

2 As you make changes to the photo, the Undo History palette tracks the steps.

3 To undo a step or multiple steps, click and drag the palette marker.

4 The photo will immediately reflect the undo—this is useful for comparing the before and after states of a multi-step fix.

correct exposures

lighten shadows

This technique works best in Standard Edit mode, where it's easier to control. We'll start here with the shadows, then fix the highlights on the next page, and if necessary, finish by tweaking the midtone contrast on page 42. (See extra bits on page 59.)

1 In our example, many details are obscured in the shadows, while a few of the brightest areas are blasted out.

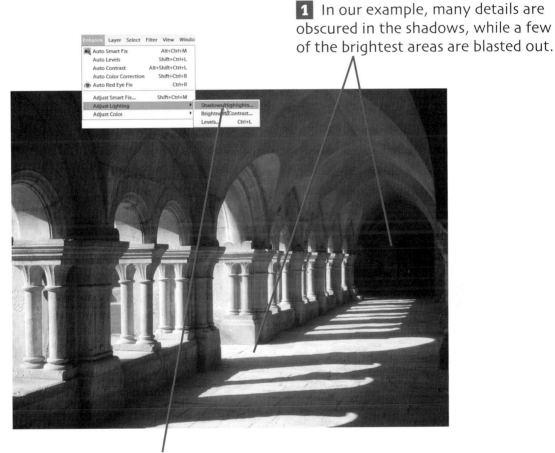

2 In Standard Edit mode, open the photo you want to fix and choose Enhance > Adjust Lighting > Shadows/Highlights.

lighten shadows (cont.)

3 When the Shadows/ Highlights dialog box opens, it immediately lightens the shadows by the default value of 25 percent. That's too much for this example.

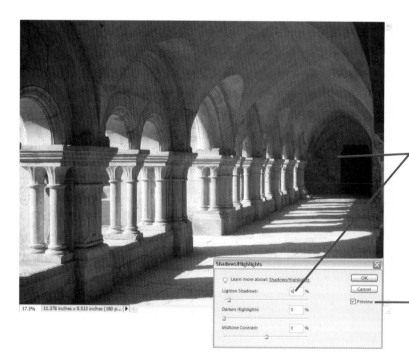

4 Move the Lighten Shadows slider left to 6, which in this case, opens up the shadows without wiping out the dramatic lighting.

5 Use the Preview checkbox to gauge what looks best. Next, we'll fix those highlights.

darken highlights

Sometimes you only need to fix the "hotspots" or highlights in a photo. But if you also need to lighten the photo's shadows, do that first, as explained in lighten shadows on pages 39–40.

1 In Standard Edit mode, open the photo you want to fix and choose Enhance > Adjust Lighting > Shadows/Highlights.

2 When the Shadows/Highlights dialog box opens, the Darken Highlights slider will be at the far left, set at 0. Drag it to the right until the very brightest areas just start to show some detail (in our example, about 15).

3 Be careful not to overcorrect the highlights. In the example, with the slider set to 100, the brightest areas show plenty of detail, but other areas look artificially lit.

We'll finish by adjusting the midtone contrast on the next page.

adjust midtones

Even when your photo has a good range of shadows and highlights, it may need a bit more "pop." You can get exactly that by adjusting the brightness of the midtones—without affecting the shadows or highlights.

Adjusting the midtone contrast too far in either direction can wreck all your previous fixes in the shadows and highlights.

In our example, we've increased the midtone contrast to +16, which preserves the natural- ness of the scene in both the darker and lighter midtones.

Save your fixes and you're done.

correct exposures

read the histogram

As we saw on the previous pages, you can make most basic exposure adjustments with just the Shadows/Highlights dialog box. But if you learn how to read the Photoshop Elements histogram, you'll have a better sense of what's wrong with a problem exposure—and how to fix it. Open the histogram by choosing Window > Histogram and it will appear in the Palette Bin. It might look a bit strange, but it's actually pretty easy to understand. Take a look at the histograms for the next four photos. (See extra bits on page 59.)

From left to right, the histogram shows the range of tones from pure black to pure white.

The top-to-bottom axis shows how much of each tone the photo contains.

This shot of a Utah canyon has few shadows, so it's not surprising that the histogram is weighted toward the right (brighter) side. But notice how the histogram stops short of reaching the far-left side. That means the photo lacks any pure black. On page 50, we'll slightly boost the contrast to improve its tonal range.

read the histogram (cont.)

Dominated by shadows, the histogram for this photo of a French cloister is almost the opposite of the canyon's.

At the far right, you do see a spike of almost pure white, representing the sky.

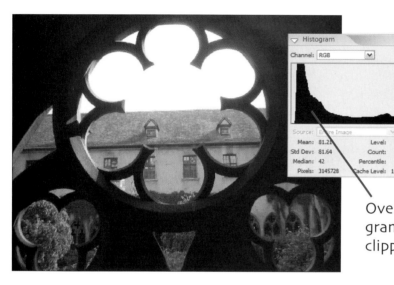

Overall, however, the histogram is skewed to the left, clipping off the black.

As the histogram shows, the photo of the two storks has a full range of tones from pure black to pure white.

On page 46, however, we'll rebalance it by reducing the contrast.

correct exposures

The flower histogram shows an almost ideal exposure: an evenly spread, full range of tones.

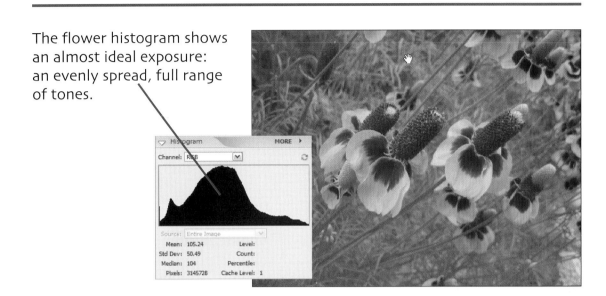

Now that you can read the histogram, let's use it to fix the stork photo.

reduce contrast

The stork photo on page 44 suffers from too much contrast, with all blacks or whites and few midtones. By watching the histogram as we use the Shadows/Highlights dialog box, we can accurately reduce the contrast.

1 Open the photo you want to fix in Standard Edit mode and make sure the histogram is visible (Window > Histogram). Choose Enhance > Adjust Lighting > Shadows/Highlights.

2 When the Shadows/Highlights dialog box opens, it automatically lightens the shadows by 50 percent.

3 The histogram's gray areas show how the photo's darkest areas were bunched up on the left before the Lighten Shadows adjustment.

4 The histogram's black areas show the new settings.

5 Because the shadows were lightened a little too much, we'll reduce the setting from 50 to 35 percent, based on some trial and error. We'll also darken the highlights by 9 percent. Most importantly, we'll reduce the Midtone Contrast by 13 percent (−13).

6 The histogram shows that the lightest areas have shifted toward the middle, and the midtones have also increased, compared to the light line marking their original levels.

7 The entire photo is less contrasty, especially in the sky and feathers.

8 While you could make these adjustments by eyeball, the histogram provides feedback that you're on the right track. Save your changes before closing the photo.

use levels

Sometimes, you may need a bit more control than the Shadows/Highlights commands can offer. That's the time to use Elements' Levels command. Take a look at the Levels dialog box for any photo by pressing Ctrl L. The changes in the example photos below are far greater than normal, just to clearly show their effects. (See extra bits on page 59.)

The Levels dialog box has its own histogram, plus sliders and text fields for adjusting a photo's brightness levels.

Before any adjustments are made, the Input Levels are set to 0, 1.00, and 255, which represent respectively the brightness/contrast levels for the shadows, midtones, and highlights.

In general, the Output Levels are seldom used to control exposure.

correct exposures

The sliders for the Input Levels control the range of tones (or contrast) in the photo by setting the values for the darkest shadows (the black point) and lightest highlights (the white point). The respective text fields can do the same with more precision.

As in Quick Fix mode, the Auto button offers a one-click-to-fix option.

The Input Levels' middle slider (and text field) control the brightness of the photo's midtones—without affecting the shadows or highlights.

The Preview button lets you compare before and after views of the changes.

Think of the middle slider (the gray one) as the base of a see-saw: Ideally, you position it so that half the histogram's volume sits to the left (the shadows) and half to the right (the highlights). Compare this photo to the one on page 48, and you'll see that the shadow area remains the same while the midtones are brighter.

correct exposures

fix levels with layers

While you can adjust the levels directly, it's much better to do it with an adjustment layer. That's because it lets you change the levels at any time without permanently tossing away any exposure information. If you change the levels directly, the changes are locked in and cannot be tweaked later. Let's see how adjusting the levels can improve the canyon photo on page 43. We'll start by boosting the contrast since the histogram shows few true blacks.

1 In Standard Edit mode, open the photo you want to fix and make sure the Histogram and Layers palettes appear in the Palette Bin (Window > Layers). Click the Adjustment Layer button and choose Levels in the drop-down menu.

2 Click OK in the dialog box that appears and the new adjustment layer will be automatically selected in the Layers palette and the Levels dialog box will open.

correct exposures

3 Reposition the Levels dialog box so that you can also see the Histogram palette, which will update as you adjust the levels.

4 Drag the black point slider right to where the Levels histogram meets the baseline.

5 Now look at the live Histogram palette and you'll see that the graph has spread to the left edge. This will adjust the previous Input Level of 12 (dark gray) to black (0) and boost the photo's tonal range and contrast.

6 Remember the notion of balancing the histogram on the middle gray slider, like a see-saw? Since we've shifted the photo's overall tonal range slightly to the right, we've also bumped the gray slider slightly right as well (from 1.0 to 1.1), which slightly brightens the midtones.

Be sure to save your work when you're done.

fix flashed-out areas

This photo shows one of the most common flash problems. The powdered sugar of the New Orleans beignet has been blasted by the flash, leaving little detail in the highlights. You can use an adjustment layer to fix it. (See extra bits on page 59.)

1 Open your flashed-out shot in Standard Edit mode and make sure the Layers palette appears in the Palette Bin (Window > Layers). Right-click the Background layer and choose Duplicate Layer from the drop-down menu.

2 Elements names the duplicate Background copy; click OK to close the dialog box and the new layer will be automatically selected in the Layers palette.

3 In the Layers palette, click the Normal drop-down menu and choose Multiply.

4 Any black in the layer is multiplied, darkening the photo overall—along with the flashed-out area. If the flashed-out area was still too bright, you could add another duplicate layer and repeat the multiply effect. Here, however, even a single duplicate layer darkens the photo too much.

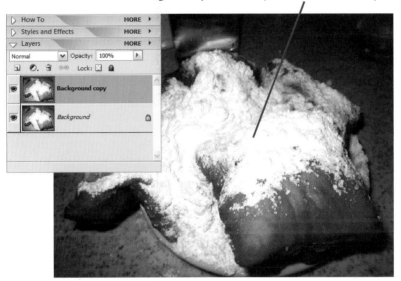

5 To adjust the amount, click the Opacity drop-down menu and drag the slider to the left.

6 In this case, after a bit of trial and error, an opacity of 77 percent looks best.

7 Save the changes when you are done.

correct exposures

add fill flash

◆NEW The yucca bloom photo shows what happens when you should use fill flash but forget: the foreground is too dark because the sky threw off the exposure. This too can be fixed using an adjustment layer, along with two tools: the new Magic Selection Brush and the related Selection Brush. (See extra bits on page 59.)

1 Open your photo in Standard Edit mode and make sure the Layers palette appears in the Palette Bin (Window > Layers). Right-click the Background layer and choose Duplicate Layer from the drop-down menu.

2 Elements names the duplicate Background copy; click OK to close the dialog box and the new layer will be automatically selected in the Layers palette.

3 With the Background copy layer still selected, select the Magic Selection Brush Tool.

4 Use the Options bar to set the brush size relatively large (42).

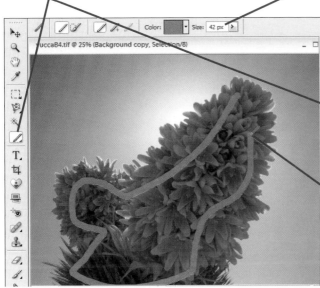

5 Drag the brush over the photo to select the general area where the exposure needs adjusting.

6 Release the cursor to trigger the selection, marked here by a dashed outline.

7 If you need to exclude any areas accidently selected—in this case a bit of sky—first magnify the unwanted area using the Zoom Tool.

add fill flash (cont.)

8 Keep the Background copy layer selected. We need more brush control to exclude that bit of sky, so in the Options bar click the Selection Brush Tool and the subtract-from-selection button.

9 Once you do, photo areas that are not part of the selection will be overlaid with a pink mask, which makes it easier to see what needs to be subtracted from the selection, such as that bit of sky.

10 Use the drop-down menu in the Options bar to choose a small brush (21-pixel diameter) with a soft, rounded-tip, which will avoid drawing a hard line between areas included and excluded (the pink) in the selection. Make several brush strokes to exclude the patch of blue sky.

11 Zoom back to a full-screen view of the photo (Ctrl 0) to see if there are any pink areas (which are not part of the selection) that need to be added.

12 Leave the Selection Brush Tool active but click the add-to-selection button. As you stroke the pink areas, they will turn blue to show that they've been added to the existing selection.

13 Zoom out for another full-screen view (Ctrl 0) to check if you're happy with the selection. With the Background copy layer still selected, right-click the adjustment layer button and select Levels.

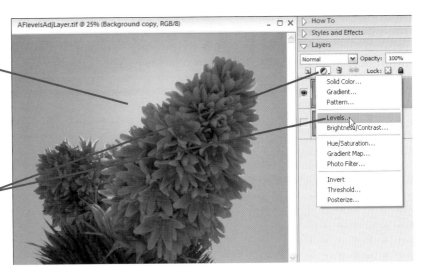

add fill flash (cont.)

14 The new adjustment layer automatically will be named Levels 1. Select the Group With Previous Layer checkbox and click OK to add the layer.

15 The Levels 1 adjustment layer becomes the top layer in the Layers palette with the white area in the mask representing the selection.

16 The Levels dialog box also opens so that you can use the sliders, especially the middle gray slider, to adjust the exposure of your selection. When you're happy with the changes, click OK to close the Levels dialog box. Having added fill flash to the photo, save your work (Ctrl S).

correct exposures

extra bits

lighten shadows p. 39

- Stay away from using the Enhance > Adjust Lighting > Brightness/Contrast control, because its changes do not distinguish between shadows, highlights, and midtones.

- It's hard to adjust the sliders precisely. Instead, click in the number text window and use the ⬆ or ⬇ keys to change the number a digit at a time. Use Shift ⬆ or Shift ⬇ to move in 10-digit steps. The Lighten Shadows and Darken Highlights sliders also appear in the Quick Fix Lighting pane—but without the text windows.

read the histogram p. 43

- To save memory, Elements does not continuously update the histogram. If a yellow triangle appears, click it to update the histogram's display.

use levels p. 48

- Because the histogram's top-to-bottom axis reflects the amount of each value, the balance point will not always fall halfway between the right and left end points.

fix flashed-out areas p. 52

- Finding the right levels often takes some trial and error. That's the great thing about adjustment layers: You can change your mind. Just double-click the adjustment layer to re-open its Levels dialog box.

add fill flash p. 54

- If you never make mistakes, you could do this without creating a copy of the Background layer. But for the rest of us, working on a copy of the layer helps avoid wiping out the original.

- Even a rough squiggle of the Magic Selection Brush Tool will usually allow it to grab what you need selected. The first time you use the brush, an explanatory dialog box will appear. Select the Don't show again checkbox and click OK to keep it from popping up constantly.

- This layer-and-brush trick works for fixing a portion of a photo. If you need to lighten the entire photo, click the Normal drop-down menu in the Layers palette and choose Screen. The steps from there are the same as fix flashed-out areas—except that it lightens instead of darkens.

4. adjust colors

Most of the time, the colors in your photos are spot on. Still, sometimes even the smartest camera gets fooled. Maybe the white balance is set for outdoors and you're inside, perhaps a flash has turned a scene cold, or nearby objects have reflected odd colors onto faces. Scanned photos or faded family shots may need some correction or rejuvenation. Before using the Standard Edit mode's color tools covered here, first try the Auto button in the Quick Fix Color palette, as explained on page 31. If you haven't already checked your monitor's settings and calibration, see page 9 before digging into this chapter.

set color management

Few things are as subjective as color perception. What's deep blue to you may look purple to me. To cope with this issue, manufacturers have created numerical color profiles for every image source (your computer, scanner, camera) and color output device (monitor or printer). Using this color management feature (sometimes called an ICC profile), Photoshop Elements embeds a color profile in each of your images. It's not perfect, but the idea is to keep colors from fluctuating as your photo moves from camera to monitor to Web page or snapshot.

In Standard Edit mode, press ⇧Shift Ctrl K to open the Color Settings dialog box. By default, No Color Management is selected. See the first extra bit on page 80 to decide which option to choose. In most cases, Always Optimize Colors for Computer Screens is best.

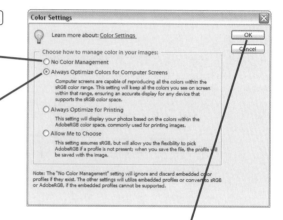

Click OK to close the dialog box and you're set. If you have a photo onscreen, you may notice an immediate, but subtle color shift.

Now, whenever you save a photo, Elements will automatically embed the chosen color profile in the file.

adjust colors

learn color basics

Take a minute to understand how colors are generated and you'll get a head start on how to adjust colors in photos. Three terms are used to describe how we perceive colors: Hue, Saturation, and Brightness, known as the HSB model of color. Hue is what most of us think of as color: red, yellow, blue, green are all different hues. Saturation refers to the vividness or purity of a particular color. Brightness, obviously, depends on how much light or dark a photo contains.

Whether it's on a computer screen or a printed page, a color photo never looks quite as rich as the real thing. That's because our eyes perceive a much greater range of hue, saturation, and brightness than any machine can reproduce. Your computer monitor tries to duplicate that range by mixing red, green, and blue light (using the RGB model) to generate all other colors. Printers take a stab at it by mixing pigments or inks of cyan, magenta, yellow, and black (using the CMYK model). While you might change colors for artistic reasons, the main point of adjusting colors is getting your monitor and/or printer to match the color you saw when you took the photo. To clearly show how hue, saturation, and brightness affect color, the sliders for the photos on this and the next page have been moved beyond the normal adjustment range in the Hue/Saturation dialog box.

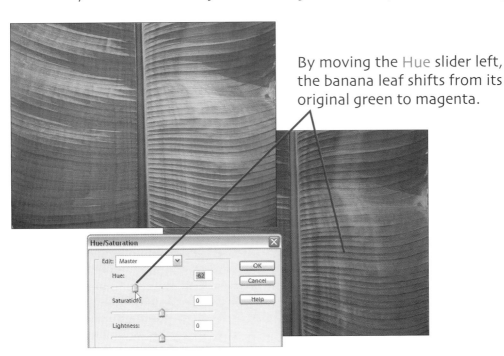

By moving the Hue slider left, the banana leaf shifts from its original green to magenta.

adjust colors

learn color basics (cont.)

Increasing the Saturation shifts the wall's original light yellow to an orange.

Greatly decreasing the saturation, the wall becomes almost black and white.

The Lightness slider works just as you'd expect: Moving the slider right lightens the photo.

Moving the slider left darkens it.

adjust colors

adjust with variations

The Color Variations feature offers a great starting point when you're still getting a feel for how hue, saturation, and brightness affect colors. It lets you compare one choice against another, making it easier to move step-by-step to the right color balance. Use this method for a while and you'll develop a good sense of how to fix a photo's color problems. (See extra bits on page 80.)

1 In Standard Edit mode, open the photo you want to fix, then from the menu bar, choose Enhance > Adjust Color > Color Variations to open the Color Variations dialog box.

2 Midtones is automatically selected, but our photo looks washed out, so we'll fix that.

3 Select Saturation and move the Amount slider left from its default middle position, just to make sure our adjustment doesn't overcorrect the saturation.

4 Click the More Saturation thumbnail and the After image will reflect the change.

5 Examine the results and, if needed, click the More Saturation thumbnail again. You can click Undo any time to move back a step.

adjust colors

6 Once you've fixed the saturation, reselect Midtones and click the thumbnail that seems to best correct the color (in this case, Decrease Red). You may need to click another thumbnail to fine-tune the adjustment.

7 Click Undo if you want to go back a step or click Reset Image if you want to start over from the beginning.

8 Once you're happy with the results, click OK to close the dialog box. Be sure to save your changes.

fix hue with layer

Just as we did with levels in the previous chapter, adjustment layers can be used to change the hue, saturation, or brightness while leaving the original photo's pixels untouched. (See extra bits on page 80.)

1 In Standard Edit mode, open the photo you want to fix and make sure the Layers palette appears in the Palette Bin (Window > Layers). Click the Adjustment Layer button and choose Hue/Saturation in the drop-down menu.

2 Click OK in the dialog box that appears and the new adjustment layer will be selected automatically in the Layers palette and the Hue/Saturation dialog box will open.

adjust colors 67

fix hue with layer (cont.)

3 Click any of the three sliders or their related text windows to adjust the setting. In this case, the Saturation was boosted to +10 and the photo shows the effect.

4 To see how the change compares to the original photo, uncheck the Preview box and the photo will return to its previous color.

5 Recheck Preview to see the fix. Once you're satisfied with the changes, click OK to close the dialog box. Be sure to save your changes.

fix skin tone with mask

By creating an adjustment layer with a mask (another overlying protective layer), we can apply color fixes to just part of a photo. This is particularly useful when, as in this example, light reflecting off the nearby hydrangeas adds a pink cast to the skin tone. We used this same method to add "fill flash" on page 54. (See extra bits on page 80.)

1 In Standard Edit mode, open your photo and make sure the Layers palette appears in the Palette Bin (Window > Layers). Right-click the Background layer and choose Duplicate Layer from the drop-down menu.

2 Elements will name the duplicate Background copy; click OK to close the dialog box and the new layer will be automatically selected in the Layers palette.

fix skin tone (cont.)

3 With the Background copy layer still selected, choose
Enhance > Adjust Color > Adjust Hue/Saturation (Ctrl U).

4 When the Hue/Saturation dialog box appears, use all
three sliders, if necessary, to adjust the skin tones to what
looks best in the photo. Don't worry if the non-skin areas
now look wrong. Click OK to close the dialog box.

5 With the Background copy layer still selected in the Layers palette, press Ctrl while clicking the New Layer button.

A new blank Layer 1 will appear between the Background and Background copy layers.

6 Select the Background copy layer again. Press Ctrl G and the Background copy layer will be grouped with Layer 1, as indicated by the downward pointing arrow. For the moment, the photo will return to its original colors. With the two layers grouped, changes to Layer 1 will affect the Background copy layer.

7 Press B to select the Brush Tool in the Toolbox, and set the foreground color to black by clicking the reset icon.

8 Use the Options Bar to select a fat brush (200-pixel diameter) with a soft, rounded tip.

adjust colors

fix skin tone (cont.)

9 In the Layers palette, make sure that the blank Layer 1 is selected.

10 Begin painting in the middle of the skin area.

11 When you're done, the middle layer will show a black area shaped like the area you painted out.

12 The layer mask blocks the face in the Background layer from appearing so that you only see the corrected skin tones in the Background copy.

Be sure to save your changes before closing the photo.

adjust colors

remove color cast

Sometimes a photo has a color cast in which even pure blacks and whites show a bit of color. When importing with a scanner, it's common for the photos to take on a slight blue cast.

When you compare the before and after versions, you realize how much color cast the original contains. In this case, the original has a slight blue-purple cast in the shadows. If you're not sure if a photo has a cast, give it a try since the technique is reversible.

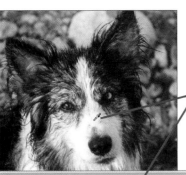

1 In Standard Edit mode, open the photo that you suspect has a color cast. Choose Enhance > Adjust Color > Remove Color Cast to open the Remove Color Cast dialog box. The cursor becomes an eye dropper that you click in a part of the photo that's supposed to be pure white or black.

2 When you click the dropper, any color cast will disappear. If nothing happens, the photo may have no cast. If the photo gains color, you didn't click on a pure black or white spot. Click Reset if you need to start over. Once you've removed the cast—or realized the photo has none—click OK. Save your changes.

remove color noise

Sometimes photos will show a lot of splotchiness in the sky or other broad patches of color, particularly if you zoom in. Called noise, this splotchiness is the digital equivalent of film grain. As with film, noise is only a problem in low light when your camera's ISO setting exceeds 150. ISO measures light sensitivity, akin to film's old ASA. To gather more light, your camera may automatically boost the ISO—or you do it manually. Either way, you can shoot in less light but at the cost of more noise. Thankfully, the noise is easy to remove. (See extra bits on page 80.)

1 In Standard Edit mode, open the problem photo and, from the menu bar, choose Filter > Noise > Reduce Noise to open the Reduce Noise dialog box. The dialog box's initial settings are applied immediately but we'll adjust them in a second.

2 First use the Hand Tool and the ⊕ or ⊖ buttons to zero in on the problem area.

3 The trick is to reduce the noise while preserving as much detail as possible. Use the Strength, Preserve Details, and Reduce Color Noise sliders to find the best compromise.

4 If your photo is formatted as a JPG/JPEG image, also try selecting the Remove JPEG Artifact checkbox.

5 Compare the before and after results by checking and unchecking the Preview box.

6 Once you're satisfied, click OK to close the dialog box. Be sure to save your changes.

warm or cool colors

Back in the days of film, photographers had to pay attention to whether they were shooting outdoors or indoors, and whether the lighting was incandescent

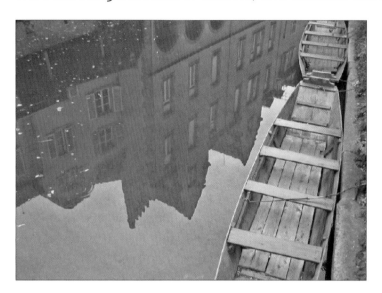

or fluorescent. Most digital cameras now have auto white balance, which handles this for you—unless you turn it off. That's one instance when you might need to warm or cool a photo's color. The example photo shows another: on a cloudy day you may need a little warmth to take the shivers off. (See extra bits on page 80.)

1 Open the problem photo in Standard Edit mode and, from the menu bar, choose Layer > New Adjustment Layer > Photo Filter. In the dialog box that appears, check Group With Previous Layer and click OK to create a new adjustment layer named Photo Filter 1. When the Photo Filter dialog box appears, Elements by default immediately applies the Warming Filter (85) at a Density of 25 percent.

2 For this example, that seems a bit too warm, so click the Filter pop-up menu and choose Warming Filter (81), which is more subdued than Warming Filter (85). If you need to cool a photo, choose one of the two cooling filters. Cooling Filter (80) is more intense (bluer) than Cooling Filter (82).

3 Once you choose the new filter, the effect appears immediately in the photo.

4 Adjust the density slider if needed.

5 Once you're satisfied, click OK to apply the change and close the dialog box. Save your changes.

adjust colors

convert colors

In a world awash with color photos, sometimes you can make an image stand out by converting it to a black-and-white shot or an old-fashioned sepia-toned photo.

1 Open the photo in Standard Edit mode and, from the menu bar, choose Enhance > Adjust Color > Remove Color. The photo will convert to a gray-scale image.

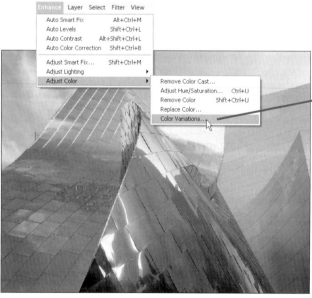

2 From the menu bar, choose Enhance > Adjust Color > Color Variations.

3 In the Color Variations dialog box, Midtones will already be selected.

4 Click the Increase Red thumbnail, then the Decrease Blue thumbnail.

5 The now sepia-toned version will appear in the After thumbnail. Tweak the other values if you like.

6 Once you're happy with your adjustments, click OK to close the dialog box. Save your changes.

adjust colors

extra bits

set color management p. 62

- The Always Optimize Colors for Computer Screens choice makes the most sense when you're creating onscreen slide shows, photos for emailing, posting on the Web, and even ordering prints online. If, however, you always create photos for your own local (desktop) printer then choose Always Optimize for Printing.

adjust with variations p. 65

- It's common to bounce between the Midtones and Saturation choices in the Color Variations dialog box.
- If you have a faded print or slide try boosting the saturation in the Variations dialog box.

fix hue with layer p. 67

- You can readjust the hue/saturation any time by double-clicking the adjustment layer.
- If you want more control, click in the number text window and use the ↑ or ↓ keys to change the number one digit at a time. Use Shift↑ or Shift↓ to move in 10-digit steps.

fix skin tone p. 69

- Feel free to try the new Enhance > Adjust Color > Adjust Color for Skin Tone feature on page 32. In this example, that feature fixed the skin tones—but skewed the color of the flowers.
- With a mask, you can adjust the color and exposure. Depending on which layer you select, you can apply color/lighting changes to the Background or Background copy.
- Depending on the photo, it may be quicker to create the layer mask using the Magic Selection Brush Tool (see page 54–55).

remove color noise p. 74

- The remove color noise feature also can be a lifesaver if you're using a low-resolution camera phone. Faces in particular can wind up looking splotchy.

warm or cool colors p. 76

- While you could apply a warming or cooling filter to the photo's Background layer, the adjustment layer preserves your original pixels.
- Whether you're warming or cooling a photo, feel free to readjust the Density slider from the standard 25 percent. For a realistic effect, keep it below 40 percent.

adjust colors

5. repair & transform photos

Repairing photos lets you restore something similar to what used to be there. Many of the same repair tools and methods also enable you to transform photos into something not seen when you snapped the picture. Some of the repair techniques require a lot of steps, but they're worth the effort because they'll give you dramatic control over all your photos.

remove dust & scratches

Dust and scratches are a constant problem any time you scan slides or prints. While this example shows dust being removed, the same method can be used for small scratches.

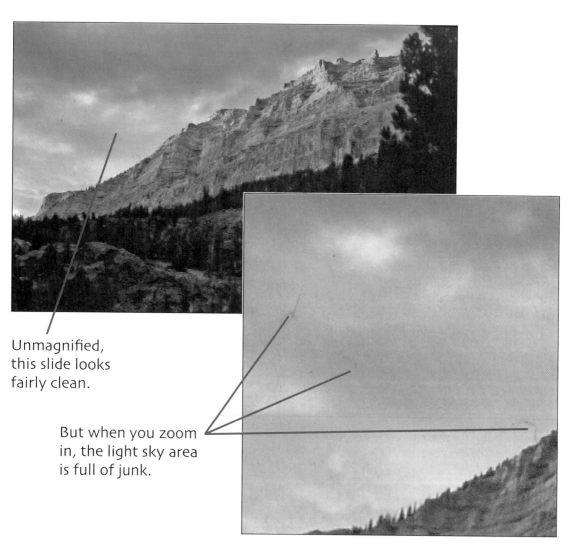

Unmagnified, this slide looks fairly clean.

But when you zoom in, the light sky area is full of junk.

repair & transform photos

While Elements includes a special filter for this (Filter > Noise > Dust & Scratches), it's applied to the entire photo. You could select only the dust areas and then apply the filter, but that's too much trouble.

1 Instead, zoom in on a problem spot in Standard Edit mode.

2 Select the Spot Healing Brush Tool.

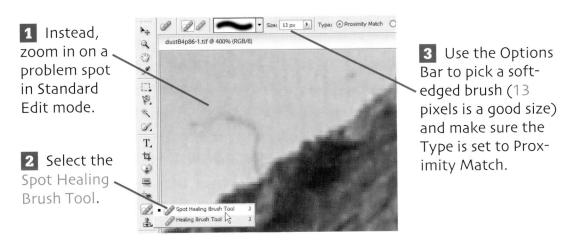

3 Use the Options Bar to pick a soft-edged brush (13 pixels is a good size) and make sure the Type is set to Proximity Match.

4 Position the brush over the dust spot (or in our example, a strand of fuzz).

5 If it's a single spot, click once. If it's a strand, as here, click and drag.

6 Release the cursor and the spot disappears into the surrounding color.

Use the Hand Tool to move to the next bit of dust and repeat the steps above until you've cleaned up all the problem areas. Save your changes.

repair & transform photos

fix blemishes

Fixing blemishes is not much different from eliminating dust spots: The Spot Healing Brush Tool is the best tool for both since you're blending a spot to match its surroundings.

1 Use the Zoom and Hand tools to get close enough to the blemish area that you can see what you're doing.

3 Use the Options Bar, pick a soft-edged brush just slightly larger than the blemish (in our example 45 pixels is a good size), and make sure the Type is set to Proximity Match.

2 Select the Spot Healing Brush Tool.

4 Position the brush over the blemish and click once. The blemish disappears as the area takes on the color of the surrounding area.

Use the Hand Tool to move to the next blemish and repeat the steps above until you've removed the most obvious spots. Save your changes.

repair areas

The Spot Healing Brush Tool performs miracles, but it has limits. Old prints, for example, often have subtle cracks in their finish, which a scanner winds up making even more apparent. The Spot Healing Brush, set to Proximity Match, would duplicate any nearby cracks, making the problem worse. If set to Create Texture, it would erase the cracks—along with all the underlying pixel variation. To repair such damage while preserving the underlying texture, your best bet is the Healing Brush Tool. (See extra bits on page 115.)

1 From the menu bar, choose View > New Window for Image, which opens a second view of the image. Use the Zoom and Hand tools to position the two windows side by side; one with a pixel-level view of the damage, the other zoomed out enough to give you an overall view of how the fix will look in the final photo.

repair areas (cont.)

2 Select the Healing Brush Tool, which shares a Toolbox berth with the Spot Healing Brush.

3 Use the Options Bar to set the brush's Diameter (fairly small, 5 pixels in our example), Hardness (23 percent is a good place to start), and leave the Mode set at Normal.

4 While pressing (Alt), click the cursor in an area with the mix of light/dark pixels you want applied to the damage. (Don't worry about matching the color; the tool will perform that magic.) The cursor turns into a cross-hair tool to help you pinpoint exactly what you're sampling. Release the cursor and (Alt) key once you've taken the sample.

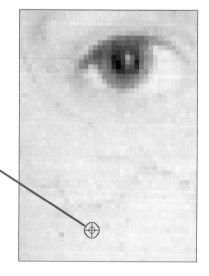

repair & transform photos

5 Position your cursor over a damaged area and click to repair it. A circle marks where the repair is being applied; a cross marks which pixels are being sampled for the fix.

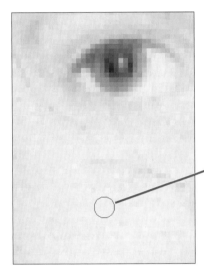

6 Continue applying the repair one click at a time, or click and drag the cursor to fix a whole line at once. When you release the cursor, it may take a second for the fix to be applied.

7 When you think you've repaired all the damaged areas, check your second zoomed-out view of the photo to be sure.

Save your changes.

restore missing areas

If half a photo is missing, you can't recreate something from nothing. But it's surprising how often you can restore smaller missing areas using the Clone Stamp Tool to duplicate nearby areas bit by bit. In the example, we start by fixing an area of uniform color, then take on a harder-to-fix striped area. (See extra bits on page 114.)

2 Use the Options Bar to pick a small soft-tip brush. In our example, a size 9 pixel brush will work well.

1 Zoom in a bit on the easier-to-fix area and select the Clone Stamp Tool in the Toolbox.

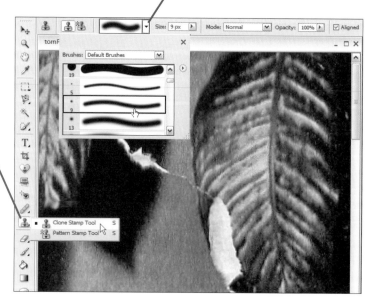

repair & transform photos

3 While pressing [Alt], click the cursor near the damage to grab a similarly colored sample.

4 Release the cursor.

5 Click on the damaged area. A circle marks where the repair is being applied; a cross marks the sample source.

6 Continue applying the sample to the damaged area, either one click at a time or in tiny brush strokes. Resample and repeat the process for other uniformly colored areas.

restore missing areas (cont.)

7 We need to get closer to restore the striped leaf, so choose View > New Window for Image to open a second view of the image. Use the Zoom and Hand tools to position a zoomed-in view next to an overall view.

8 Use the Options Bar to pick a brush with a fuzzy tip in a larger size (21 pixels in our example).

9 While pressing (Alt), click the cursor in the middle of a striped leaf.

10 Release the cursor.

11 Align your brush tip with the middle of the stripe but extending into the blank area. Its reach will be indicated by a 21-pixel-wide circle—the diameter of the Clone Stamp Tool's brush. Click once and the stripe will be applied to the blank area.

12 Use the cross marking the sample source to keep the brush aligned with the middle of the stripe. Continue painting into the blank area one click at a time. Stop short of the opposite edge of the blank area.

13 While pressing [Alt], grab a sample of the next stripe.

14 Repeat the process of extending the stripe out into the blank area.

restore missing areas (cont.)

15 Once you've filled in the main area, select a smaller brush and continue using the Clone Stamp Tool to patch details along the edge.

16 When you think you've repaired all the damaged areas, check the zoomed-out view to be sure. If not, zoom back in and finish up any repairs with the Clone Stamp Tool.

17 Save your changes.

repair & transform photos

select part of photo

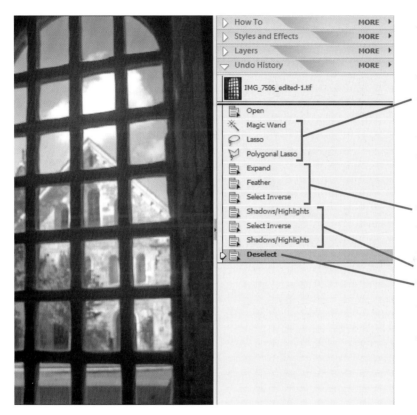

NEW Elements offers five tools for selecting parts of a photo—the Marquee, Lasso, Magic Wand, Selection Brush, and the new Magic Selection Brush. Once a selection's made, it can be deleted, copied, or changed without affecting the rest of the photo. (For details on using the Magic Selection Brush, see pages 55–57.)

As the Undo History palette for this photo shows, it's common to use a combination of selection tools. Once you've selected an area, you then apply various commands to expand, shrink, or reverse the selection. In the typical retouching session, you then apply several fixes before finally deselecting the area. Trial and error soon shows you which tools and methods suit your style.

select part of photo (cont.)

With the circle-version of the Marquee Tool set to Fixed Aspect Ratio, it's easy to select the round logo on this German telephone booth.

You can then apply such transformations as Image > Transform > Free Transform to pivot the circle open like a window.

With the Magic Wand Tool set for a wide range of color (Tolerance 64) in a single area (Contiguous), you can quickly select the block of blue-purple hyacinths.

Then you can use the Shadows/ Highlights dialog box to lighten only that color.

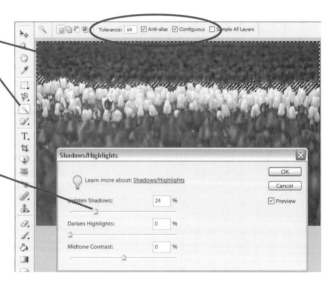

repair & transform photos

With the Selection Brush Tool set for a large brush with a very defined tip (Size 19 pixels), you can just brush over an area to select it. In this example of extreme red eye, however, Elements may have met its match.

All three variations of the Lasso Tool work by drawing a loop around an area to select it. While it can be as tricky to use as double-sided tape, the Magnetic Lasso works well for laying a line down along the irregular edge in the example.

modify selection

After selecting part of a photo, it's easy to modify that selection. You add to the selection or remove some of it. The Select menu lets you change the boundary between the selection and the rest of the photo.

All the selection tools let you add to your selection by using the tool while pressing [Shift].

You can remove from the selection while using the tool by pressing [Alt].

To change the boundary of a selection, choose Select > Modify and pick from the drop-down menu.

Our cookie selection with the Magnetic Lasso was a little ragged, so we choose Select > Modify > Smooth. A dialog box controls the amount of smoothing.

Having smoothed the selection, we want to soften its edge by choosing Select > Feather.

When you choose Select > Feather, a dialog box controls the width of the feathering in pixels.

Set to 0 pixels leaves a distinct boundary,...

...10 pixels blurs it a bit,...

...and 50 pixels creates a very soft edge.

Sometimes it's much easier to select what you don't want and then reverse the selection. To adjust the exposure outside the window, for example, would require selecting each pane of glass.

Instead, use the Magic Wand to select the surrounding black, then choose Select > Inverse.

That reverses the selection to the view outside.

remove objects

The Healing Brush and Clone Stamp examples earlier in the chapter gave you a sense of how easy it might be to remove objects in a photo. With your new selection skills, we'll start small by removing some distracting wires. (See extra bits on page 114.)

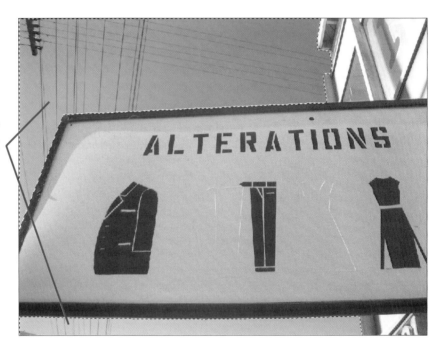

1 To ensure we don't remove any of the sign, select the sky above and below it.

2 Choose Select > Save Selection so that all your work making the selection doesn't disappear with the click of a wrong key.

3 Name the selection and click OK to close the dialog box.

98   **repair & transform photos**

4 Choose the Clone Stamp Tool.

5 Set the brush tip small enough to work amid the wires (13 pixels is a good size), then [Alt]-click to grab a sample of the sky. Release the cursor.

6 Start erasing the wires one click at a time. A circle marks where the stamp is applied; a cross marks the sample source. Because only the sky's selected, we can click right up to the sign without turning it blue.

remove objects (cont.)

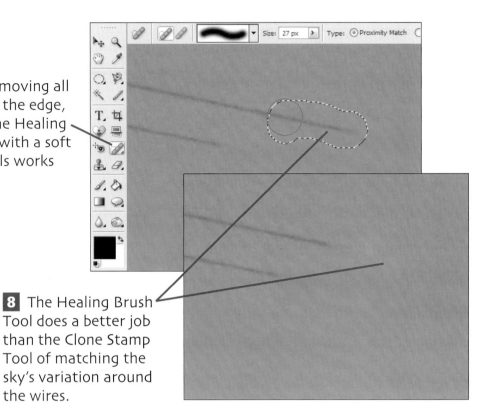

7 After removing all wires along the edge, switch to the Healing Brush Tool with a soft tip (27 pixels works well here).

8 The Healing Brush Tool does a better job than the Clone Stamp Tool of matching the sky's variation around the wires.

Though it takes time, the final photo shows no sign of the previous tangle of wires.

ALTERATIONS

extract & defringe objects

NEW In the previous section, we carefully removed just the wires while preserving the blue sky. But suppose, we wanted to remove all the sky and work only with the remaining sign and building? The new Magic Extractor is perfect for that sort of task, especially since it includes a Defringe option to automatically remove the boundary fringe of pixels often mistakenly selected with an object. (See extra bits on page 114.)

1 Open a photo from which you want to extract a particular area. In our example, we'll start by opening the same wire-free photo we created on pages 98–100. Choose Image > Magic Extractor and the image appears within the Magic Extractor dialog box.

2 The Foreground Brush Tool will be selected by default with a Brush Size of 20 pixels.

3 Click within the photo on all the areas you want to add to your selection. Each of the areas will be marked by a red dot.

extract & defringe (cont.)

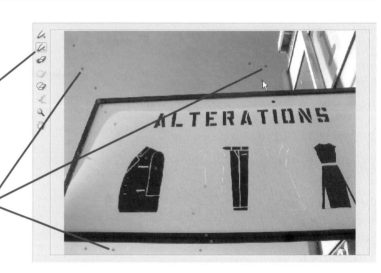

4 Now select the Background Brush Tool, leave the Brush Size as is, and click on the areas you want to place outside (subtract from) the selection. These areas will be marked by blue dots. Click Preview to start the extraction.

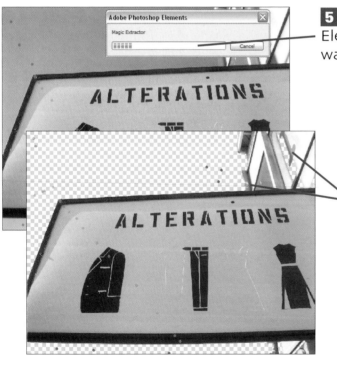

5 A progress bar will appear as Elements extracts the area you want from the rest of the photo.

6 When the extraction's finished, check to see if any areas were mistakenly left out or included in your selection.

repair & transform photos

7 Use the Zoom Tool (🔍) to zero in on areas missed in your initial selection. (If the only problem involves a small fringe of pixels around the object, skip to step 11.)

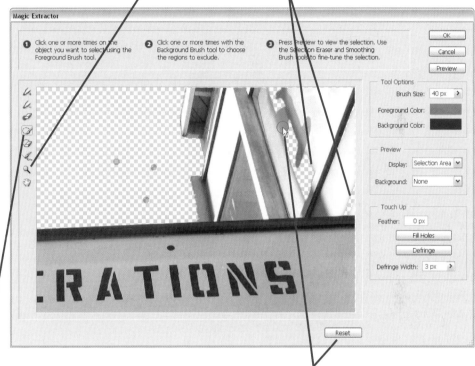

8 Select the Add to Selection Tool (🖌) and choose a Brush Size that's big enough to quickly cover the missing areas and small enough to not spill into adjacent areas. In our example, 40 pixels seems about right.

9 Use the tool to paint in any areas you want to add to the selection. If you ever want to start from scratch in creating the selection, click Reset.

10 If the Magic Extractor picks up any areas you do not want included in the selection, select the Remove from Selection Tool (🖌), choose a Brush Size, and paint in any areas you want to subtract from the selection.

repair & transform photos

extract & defringe (cont.)

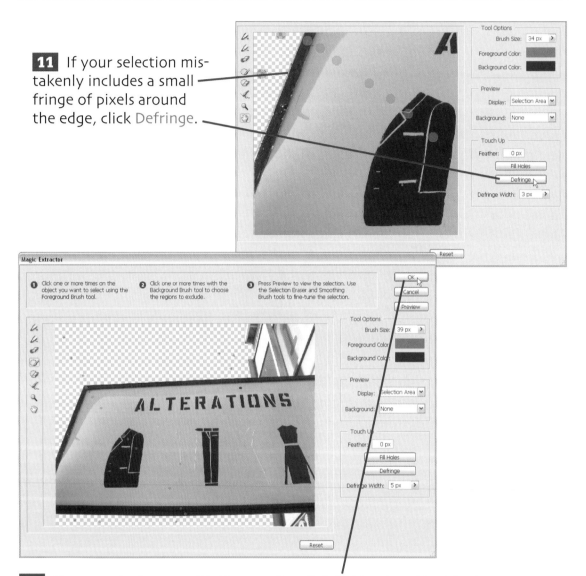

11 If your selection mistakenly includes a small fringe of pixels around the edge, click Defringe.

12 Once you're happy with the results, click OK to close the Magic Extractor dialog box and return to the Standard Edit main window. Be sure to save your work ((Ctrl) (S)). We'll use this same photo in the next section and fill the transparent areas with pixels from another photo.

combine photos

Using layers, we're going to move items from one photo to another. It takes a lot of steps. But, once you master this method, you can combine bits and pieces from multiple images in a single photo. (See extra bits on page 114.)

1 Open the photo to which you want to add items from another photo. Our example is the same alterations sign we used in the previous section.

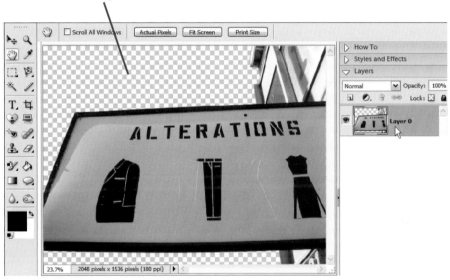

combine photos (cont.)

2 Switch to your second photo and select what you want to move to the first photo, in this case a more dramatic sky.

3 Choose Layer > New > Layer via Copy.

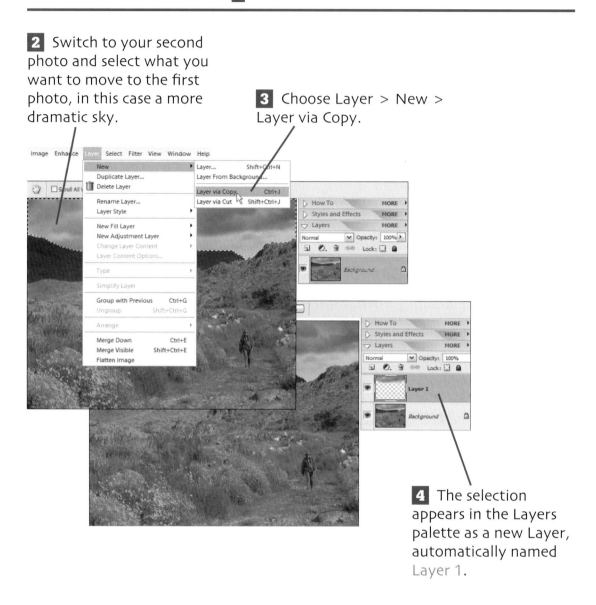

4 The selection appears in the Layers palette as a new Layer, automatically named Layer 1.

repair & transform photos

5 Use the Photo Bin to bring up the still-open first photo. Position the windows so that the first photo is visible right below the second photo.

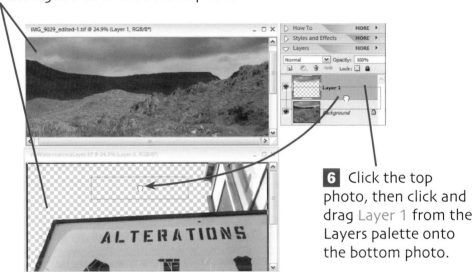

6 Click the top photo, then click and drag Layer 1 from the Layers palette onto the bottom photo.

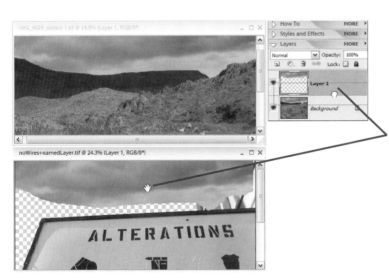

7 Release the cursor and Layer 1 will be pasted into the bottom photo. It also will appear in the Layers palette. Minimize or close the other photo to give you more room to work.

repair & transform photos 　　　　　　　　　　　　　**107**

combine photos (cont.)

8 Click the Move Tool in the Toolbox (or press V).

9 A dashed line borders the new layer, with square "handles" at its corners and sides.

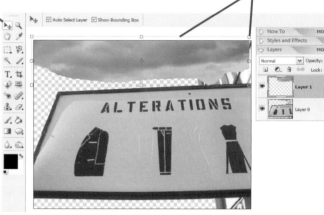

10 Click and drag the various side and corner handles to fit Layer 1 over the transparent area.

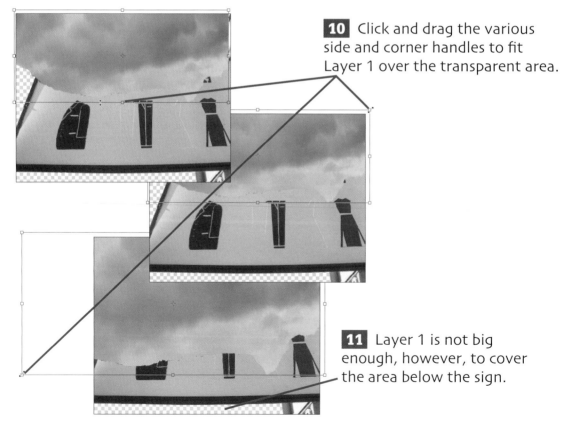

11 Layer 1 is not big enough, however, to cover the area below the sign.

repair & transform photos

12 Instead, right-click Layer 1 and choose Duplicate Layer.

13 The duplicate will be named Layer 1 copy. Click OK to close the dialog box.

14 The duplicate layer will appear in the Layers palette.

15 To see the original image, click and drag Layer 0 to the top of the Layers palette.

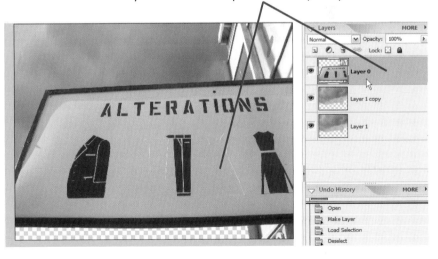

combine photos (cont.)

16 Select Layer 1 copy in the Layers palette, then click the Move Tool in the Toolbox (or press V).

17 Use the ↓ key to shift Layer 1 copy down enough to cover the area below the sign. (Don't click on the image or you'll wind up reselecting the visible Layer 0.) A dashed line marks the edge of the layer as it moves down the image.

18 A bit of brighter sky mars the effect, but that's easy to fix.

19 Click and drag Layer 1 copy to the bottom of the Layers palette. This puts it beneath Layer 1, blocking out the lighter area to create a seamless new sky.

20 Merge the layers by choosing Layer > Flatten Image. Save your changes (Ctrl S).

repair & transform photos

create a panorama

Nothing puts the viewer into a scene more dramatically than a panorama photo. Many digital cameras include features to help you create a panoramic picture by overlapping a series of photos. Photoshop Elements' Photomerge feature then takes those multiple photos and stitches them into a single photo.

1 In Standard Edit mode, open the photos with which you'll build the panorama (Ctrl O). Or use the Elements Organizer and its tags to find what you need, then choose Go to Standard Edit from the Edit drop-down menu.

2 After the photos open in Standard Edit mode, position them so you can compare their exposure and color. Fix any differences now—before you start creating the panorama.

create a panorama (cont.)

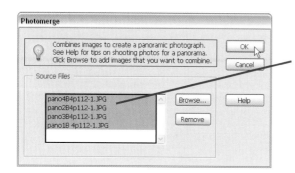

3 Choose File > New > Photomerge Panorama to open the Photomerge dialog box. The open photos will be listed in the dialog box, but you must select each one before clicking OK.

4 If Elements cannot merge all the photos, it puts the leftover images at the top.

5 Click and drag the first leftover photo to the correct spot in the panorama.

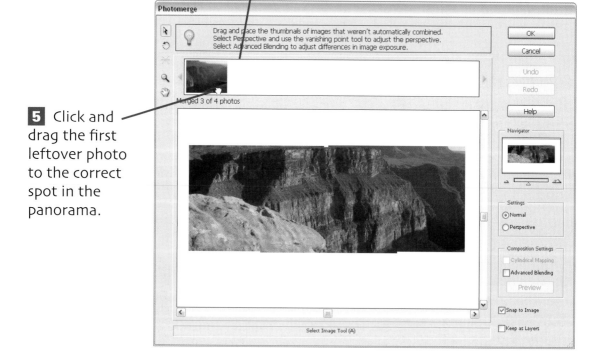

6 You don't need to be that precise when you drag the image into place. It will jump into position because Snap to Image is checked by default.

7 Drag any remaining photos into place and click OK.

8 If the original pictures were not perfectly aligned, there may be some ragged borders in the panorama image. Clean them up with the Crop Tool.

The panorama is a new file, so be sure to save your work.

extra bits

repair areas p. 85

- In picking a Healing Brush size, remember: the larger the flaw, the bigger the brush.
- As you move around the photo and repair areas, use (Alt)-click to grab new pixel samples nearer the area being fixed.

restore missing areas p. 88

- Though the example is black and white, the same steps apply working with full-color photos.
- When you change the brush size, stay with a fuzzy tip so each click/stroke blends well.

remove objects p. 98

- To paint out an object wider than the Healing Brush Tool's tip, switch to the Clone Stamp Tool. The Healing Brush tries to blend the object with the surrounding color, making a mess.
- The same methods can add objects to a photo. It's just a matter of what you sample.

extract & defringe p. 101

- Avoid starting over by using the Point Eraser Tool to remove dots placed by the Foreground Brush Tool or Background Brush Tool.
- The Touch Up pane's Feather and Defringe options work in opposite ways: Feather expands the boundary of your selection while Defringe shrinks it.
- Start with a Defringe Width of 3 pixels. If that doesn't fix the problem, increase the width and click Defringe again.

combine photos p. 105

- If the Background layer shows a lock in the Layers palette, you must unlock it to add transparent areas: Double-click the layer and click OK in the New Layer dialog box to unlock the layer.
- You also must unlock the Background layer to change its order in the Layers palette. The layer order works like a stack of windows. Transparent portions of the upper layers let you see any layers beneath them; solid portions on top block the appearance of those below.
- To reposition the bounding box, click and drag the red crosshair.

6. share photos

The payoff for all that work fixing your photos comes when you can share them with friends and relatives. Some of them will want prints, others will prefer to see them on a computer screen. Either way, Elements makes it easy.

print photos

Printing photos with Elements couldn't be easier: Open the photo or photos you want to print, choose File > Print, pick a size, and click Print.

But Elements also has a less-obvious, paper-saving option called the Picture Package, which lets you print different-sized photos on a single sheet. You can use the same photo or several photos. Either way, you wind up with a photo package akin to those offered by school and wedding photographers. (See extra bits on page 129.)

Open the photo or photos you want to print in Quick Fix or Standard Edit mode and choose File > Print Multiple Photos. In the Print Photos dialog box, your open photos run down the left.

Choose Picture Package and the center layout will reflect the choice.

Choose a photo-layout combination. (In our example, a 4 x 6 print of three different photos will appear on a single letter-sized sheet.)

If you like, you can select a fanciful frame for the photos.

If you want multiple, but different-sized, copies of the same photo on the same page of paper, check Fill Page With First Photo. Use the first drop-down menu in the Select a Layout section to choose a mix of photo sizes. In our example, that change means we'll have two 4 x 5 prints, two 2.5 x 3.5 prints, and four 2 x 2.5 prints of the same image on a single page. The same mix of sizes will be used for the other two images, using a total of three sheets of paper.

If you're printing multiple sheets, click the arrows to see the other sheets. Here, the third sheet shows the same mix of sizes for the third photo. Once you've set your combination, click Print.

set email preference

When preparing to email photos, the Preferences dialog box in Elements offers you four choices. Each is explained below. Try several to discover which works best for you.

1 Start by setting the email preferences for Elements. If you are working in the Editor (in Quick Fix or Standard Edit mode), choose Edit > Preferences > Organize & Share. If you're working in the Organizer, choose Edit > Preferences > Sharing.

2 In the Preferences dialog box, select Sharing. (If you were in the Organizer, it already will be selected.) Choose an E-mail client from the drop-down menu.

3 If you choose Outlook Express, Elements automatically attaches photos to a blank outgoing Outlook message.

Choosing Adobe E-mail Service creates a message that's sent by Elements itself. If you decide to use the Adobe service, make sure you're connected to the Internet, fill in your name and email address, and see the next step.

The Save to Hard Disk choice stores the converted photo on your computer for sending manually with any email program.

Once you make a choice from the drop-down menu, click OK to close the dialog box.

4 If you choose the Adobe E-Mail Service, Elements automatically asks you to re-confirm your email address by entering a special code that's sent to you by email.

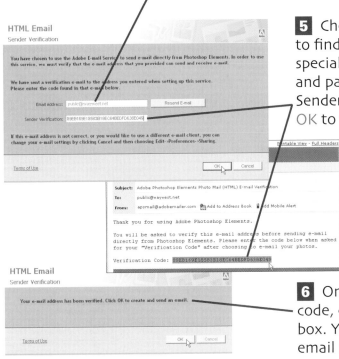

5 Check your email program to find the message and copy the special code. Return to Elements and paste the code into the Sender Verification field. Click OK to finish the verification.

6 Once Elements confirms your code, click OK to close the dialog box. You're ready to begin sending email right from Elements.

7 After setting the preferences, open the photo(s) you want to send. If you are working in the Editor (Quick Fix or Standard Edit), click the email icon in the shortcuts bar. Elements then switches to the Organizer. If you're already working in the Organizer, click the Share icon in the shortcuts bar and choose E-mail.

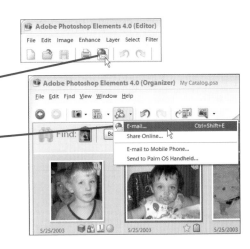

8 The appearance of the Attach to E-mail dialog box varies, depending on your choice in step 3.

send as attachments

If you chose Save to Hard Disk on page 118, the Attach to E-mail dialog box lets you adjust the size and quality of the photos that will be attached.

1 If you want to attach more photos, click Add.

2 The Add Photos dialog box lets you quickly look through and choose photos from your entire catalog or using particular tags and collections. Once you narrow your search on the left, check individual boxes to the left of the photos or use the Select All button. Click Done to close the dialog box and the selected photos appear in the Attach to E-mail dialog box.

3 In the Attach to E-mail dialog box, click Next and you'll see that the photo(s) are saved in a separate folder. Click OK to close that dialog box and then use the email program of your choice to send the photos.

share photos

use Adobe service

If you chose the Adobe E-mail Service on page 118, Elements offers you two choices. The plainer option (described below) lets you send photos as individual attachments. The fancier option (described on page 122) allows you to insert photos right into the body of your message and apply special text formats.

1 Leave Format set to Individual Attachments.

2 Choose recipients from the list.

3 Add new recipients by clicking Edit Contacts and using the dialog box that appears.

4 To attach more photos, click Add (see step 2 on the previous page).

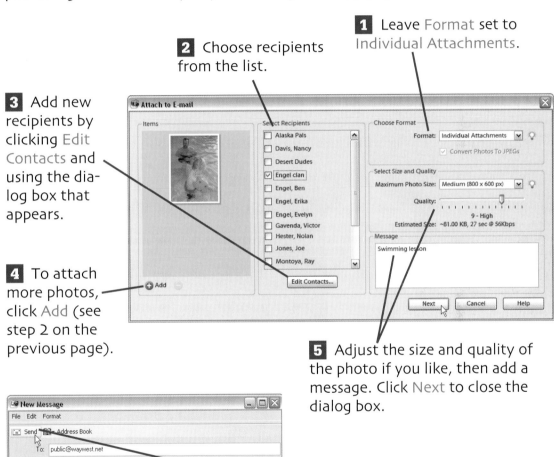

5 Adjust the size and quality of the photo if you like, then add a message. Click Next to close the dialog box.

6 The New Message dialog box appears; this gives you the option of formatting your text. When you're done, click Send and Elements dispatches the message.

use Adobe service (cont.)

NEW If you chose the Adobe E-mail Service on page 118, Elements also lets you use photo mail (or HTML mail as it's sometimes called). It allows you to insert photos directly in the body of your message instead of as separate attachments. You also can add decorative backgrounds or icons and apply fancy text formatting. (See extra bits on page 129.)

1 Make sure you've already set your email preferences. (See steps 1–4 for email photos on page 120.) Open the photo(s) you want to send, and if you are working in the Editor (Quick Fix or Standard Edit), click the email icon in the shortcuts bar. If you're already working in the Organizer, click the Share icon in the shortcuts bar and choose E-mail.

2 When the Attach to E-mail dialog box appears, use the Add button to gather any additional photos you want to include. (See step 10 page 120.) Then click the Format drop-down menu and choose Photo Mail (HTML). Click Next to close the dialog box.

3 In the Stationery & Layouts Wizard, scroll through the list of stationery styles to find one to your liking. Click Next Step.

4 Customize your layout by selecting the Photo Size and Layout for your photos.

5 Skip the Text section since you can change that later. Finally, check any options you want applied, such as drop shadows. Click Next.

use Adobe service (cont.)

6 The New Message dialog box shows exactly how your photos will appear in the email. Select any text you want to edit, then use the formatting bar to change any fonts, styles, etc.

7 Once you're satisfied with the message and its formatting, click Send. The New Message dialog box closes and the Attach to E-mail dialog box reappears briefly before also closing and returning you to the Organizer.

8 A progress bar appears briefly as Elements prepares the message. Finally another smaller progress bar appears as the message and its photos are actually mailed.

save for the web

Posting photos on a Web page is a great way to share them. When you make prints, you try to preserve every last detail to get the most faithful photo reproduction. But when you prepare an image for the Web, it's almost the opposite: You try to slim the file down so it will download quickly to the viewer's computer. The slimming process is called optimization, and the Save For Web dialog box makes it easy. (See extra bits on page 129.)

1 In Quick Fix or Standard Edit mode, open the photo you want to use on the Web and choose File > Save for Web. The photo appears in the Save For Web dialog box.

2 By default, the photo opens at 100 percent, so use the Hand Tool to maneuver the main part of your photo into view.

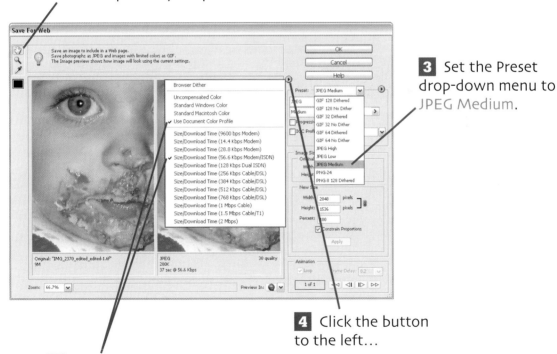

3 Set the Preset drop-down menu to JPEG Medium.

4 Click the button to the left...

5 ...and make two selections in the drop-down menu: Use Document Color Profile and Size/Download Time (56.6 Kbps Modem/ISDN).

save for the web (cont.)

6 Check two more boxes: Progressive and ICC Profile.

7 Listed at the bottom left is the photo's present size in the TIFF format (in this case 9 megabytes). To the right is its size (204.4 bytes) as a JPEG file and how long it would take to download (38 seconds at 56.6 Kbps) if we click OK.

8 But wait, even though the format's different, the dimensions of the original and the new version remain the same: 2048 x 1536. Since the new version is going to be on a Web page, it could be a lot smaller. Otherwise, you'll wind up with a giant screen-filling photo, like this cake fan's face.

9 Use the Zoom drop-down menu to find a setting closer to how large you want the photo to appear on the Web page. In our example, a Zoom setting of 12.5 percent looks about right.

10 In the New Size panel, type 12.5 into the Percent box and click Apply.

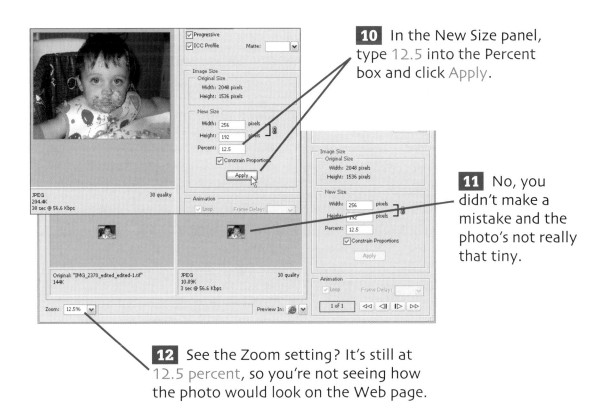

11 No, you didn't make a mistake and the photo's not really that tiny.

12 See the Zoom setting? It's still at 12.5 percent, so you're not seeing how the photo would look on the Web page.

save for the web (cont.)

13 Set the Zoom level back to 100 percent and you can see exactly how big the photo will appear on the Web.

14 The New Size panel lists its physical dimensions at 256 x 192 pixels. That's 3.5 x 2.6 inches—just about right for viewing on a computer screen.

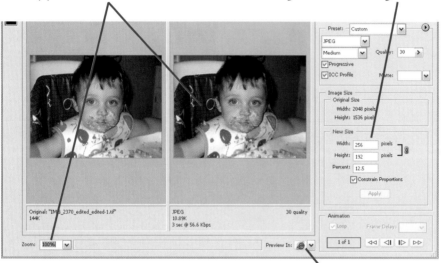

15 If you're still skeptical, click the Preview In button. Your Web browser launches and shows how the photo will look on the Web.

16 Click OK to save the optimized image. Name it, pick where to store it, and click Save. It will not affect your original photo. You'll need a Web program to upload the new image.

share photos

extra bits

print photos p. 116

- If a dialog box appears and warns that the image will print at less than 220 dpi (dots per inch), the printer probably is still set to print letter-sized documents. Choose File > Page Setup and in the Page Setup dialog box click the Printer and then Properties buttons to check and change the settings.

use Adobe service p. 121

- To thwart spam, a few people set their Web browsers and email programs to block the display of HTML-based graphics. Any email you send them will appear without fancy text formats and the photos will be included as plain attachments.

save for the web p. 125

- You can trim so much digital fat from a Web-bound photo because of the difference between printers and computer monitors. For a print to look good, printers need to lay down at least 150 dots per inch (dpi). Photos on a monitor, however, look great at just 72–96 dpi. For onscreen Web pages, the rest of those dots can be tossed, during optimization.

- Your Size/Download Time choice doesn't change the photo in any way. It simply helps you gauge how long a viewer will have to wait to see your image.

- Choosing Progressive in the Save For Web dialog box helps Web surfers with slow connection speeds see a sketchy version of the photo as it downloads. That way they can decide if they want to wait for the whole picture or move on to another page.

- Choosing ICC in the Save For Web dialog box embeds color profile data in the photo—making it easier for other profile-enabled computers to display the photo properly.

- If you haven't set a default Web browser, Elements will show you how to set one when you click Preview In.

- If anyone tried to print out the Web image of the baby's face, it would be postage-stamp size. That's the difference between the resolution of a computer screen (72 or 96 dpi) and a photo print (150–300 dpi). To post photos for prints, use your Web-site creation software to create a separate download link to the big original file.

index

index